Legislators and Representation in Sri Lanka

Westview Special Studies

The concept of Westview Special Studies is a response to the continuing crisis in academic and informational publishing. Library budgets are being diverted from the purchase of books and used for data banks, computers, micromedia, and other methods of information retrieval. Interlibrary loan structures further reduce the edition sizes required to satisfy the needs of the scholarly community. Economic pressures on university presses and the few private scholarly publishing companies have greatly limited the capacity of the industry to properly serve the academic and research communities. As a result, many manuscripts dealing with important subjects, often representing the highest level of scholarship, are no longer economically viable publishing projects--or, if accepted for publication, are typically subject to lead times ranging from one to three years.

Westview Special Studies are our practical solution to the problem. As always, the selection criteria include the importance of the subject, the work's contribution to scholarship, and its insight, originality of thought, and excellence of exposition. We accept manuscripts in camera-ready form, typed, set, or word processed according to specifications laid out in our comprehensive manual, which contains straightforward instructions and sample pages. The responsibility for editing and proofreading lies with the author or sponsoring institution, but our editorial staff is always available to answer questions and provide guidance.

The result is a book printed on acid-free paper and bound in sturdy, library-quality soft covers. We manufacture these books ourselves using equipment that does not require a lengthy make-ready process and that allows us to publish first editions of 300 to 1000 copies and to reprint even smaller quantities as needed. Thus, we can produce Special Studies quickly and can keep even very specialized books in print as long as there is a demand for them.

About the Book and Author

Focusing on the work of Sri Lankan legislators, this book offers a unique model of representation useful in examining parliamentary systems, especially those found in the Third World. Dr. Oberst explores the legislator's role in the planning and implementation of development projects, an increasingly important part of Sri Lankan legislators' responsibilities as the country seeks to decentralize its development planning. He also discusses other areas of the legislators' involvement, including constituency service (largely employment counseling) and law-making.

Robert C. Oberst is assistant professor of political science at Nebraska Wesleyan University.

Legislators and Representation in Sri Lanka
The Decentralization of Development Planning

Robert C. Oberst

Westview Press / Boulder and London

Westview Special Studies on South and Southeast Asia

All rights reserved. No part of this publication may be reproduced or transmitted in any form or by any means, electronic or mechanical, including photocopy, recording, or any information storage or retrieval system, without permission in writing from the publisher.

Copyright © 1985 by Westview Press, Inc.

Published in 1985 in the United States of America by Westview Press, Inc., 5500 Central Avenue, Boulder, Colorado 80301; Frederick A. Praeger, Publisher

Library of Congress Cataloging in Publication Data
Oberst, Robert.
   Legislators and representation in Sri Lanka.
   (Westview special studies on South and Southeast Asia)
(A Westview special study)
   Bibliography: p.
   Includes index.
   1. Legislators--Sri Lanka. 2. Representative government and representation--Sri Lanka. 3. Economic development and projects--Sri Lanka. I. Title. II. Series.
JQ657.023 1985   328.549'3073   85-3244

Composition for this book was provided by the author
Printed and bound in the United States of America

10 9 8 7 6 5 4 3 2 1

Dedicated to

Kathy

Contents

	Page
LIST OF TABLES	xi
LIST OF FIGURES	xii
PREFACE	xiii

Chapter

1. INTRODUCTION 1
2. SRI LANKAN SOCIETY AND POLITICS 11
3. LEGISLATIVE ATTITUDES 23
4. POLITICAL DEMANDS 33
5. CONSTITUENCY SERVICE 55
6. LAW-MAKING AND REPRESENTATION 73
7. DEVELOPMENT WORK 97
8. SUMMARY 121
9. IS PARLIAMENT OF VALUE? 133

APPENDIX 143
BIBLIOGRAPHY 145
INDEX 153

Tables and Figures

TABLES   Page

2.1 Distribution of members interviewed by province. 12
2.2 Distribution of MPs interviewed by party . . . 12
2.3 Ethnic population of Sri Lanka 14
2.4 Religious composition of the Sri Lankan population. 15
2.5 Party positions following the elections of 1970 and 1977. 19
3.1 Time use by MPs in different aspects of job 25
3.2 Primary use of time by MPs and formal authority in parliament 25
3.3 Important aspects of job among all members 26
3.4 Most important aspect of job and formal authority in parliament 27
3.5 Use of time and importance of aspects of job among the "rebels" 29
3.6 Congruence between most important aspect of job and main use of time 29
4.1 Average days spent by MPs in electorate per month 35
4.2 Main reasons why constituents come to MPs as cited by MPs 36
4.3 Secondary reasons cited by MPs for constituents coming to them 36
4.4 Constituent reasons for coming to meet with members in observed meetings 37
4.5 Local organisations cited by members 42
5.1 Average number of constituents meeting with MPs per week 57
5.2 Average number of constituents seen per week by MPs 59
5.3 Policy influence of ministers and number of constituents coming. 59
5.4 Patronage power and number of constituents coming. 59

		Page
5.5	Formal authority and amount of mail received per week.	61
5.6	Legislator's attitudes about meetings with constituents.	68
5.7	Legislator's attitudes about meetings with constituents and formal authority	68
5.8	Average number of constituents coming to meet with MPs per week and attitudes about their role in meeting with them.	69
6.1	Number of bills introduced by ministries from September 1978 to July 1979	75
6.2	Number of bills introduced by ministries from June 1970 to November 1971.	76
6.3	Members' attitudes toward the consultative committees	83
6.4	Questions asked by party.	87
6.5	Focus of questions asked.	87
6.6	Average number of columns of debate and formal authority	90
6.7	Columns of debate and ministers divided by number of bills introduced to parliament	91
6.8	Average columns of debate with rebels and ministers divided by bills presented to parliament.	91
7.1	Average Seventh Parliament DCB total allocations by party, formal authority and year	101
7.2	Average Eighth Parliament continuing allocations by party, formal authority and year	102
7.3	Method of selection of projects under DCB.	105
7.4	Formal authority and method of selection of projects under DCB.	105
7.5	Major organizations consulted by MPs.	105
7.6	Groups consulted and formal authority in parliament.	106
7.7	Per capita allocations of first MP.	112
7.8	Per capita allocations of second MP	113
7.9	Average percent of DCB allocations spent by MPs	117

FIGURES

4.1	Types of demands made on legislators.	34
4.2	Frequency of demands made on legislators.	44

Preface

This is an attempt to examine a largely forgotten subject of Third World politics--legislatures. At the time the research was undertaken, there had been few studies of the Sri Lankan legislature. One of the few attempts to study legislators in Sri Lanka had resulted in near failure because of the lack of cooperation of the legislators (Singer, 1964). The initial fears of a similar conclusion to this study were soon shattered by the high degree of cooperation shown by the Sri Lankan MPs. Although a few refused to be interviewed, those who did went beyond the limits of politeness in their cooperation and candor. It is these men and women who made this study possible. I hope that I have done them justice. I have tried to protect their annonymity to avoid any potential embarrassment which might result from their remarks.

The original research for this project was carried out under a grant from the Shell foundation of London which provided funding for travel and living expenses in Sri Lanka. In addition, the assistance of Edward Donovan and Bogoda Premaratne of the United States Educational Foundation in Colombo was instrumental in providing an open environment to carry out the research. There are few countries in the world where a foreigner can enter the country, gain access to its leaders, and snoop around asking sensitive questions of its leaders. I must acknowledge the uniqueness of the Sri Lankan government for allowing its many good and bad points to be exposed to a stranger from another country. I have not intended to harm any person or political group in the country. I hope that those who may have expected me to make statements favorable to them or to acknowledge them are not disappointed if I have failed to follow through with their expectations.

In a study of this nature there are many people who deserve to be acknowledged and thanked for their contribution to the final product. My wife Kathy Shellogg has had to endure my frustrations and the many hours spent in the office preparing the manuscript. Her advice and editorial help have been invaluable. However, there is one person without whose assistance and help this book would never have appeared. Robert N. Kearney provided many hours of his time criticising and advising about the many drafts this work went through from its original design to the final product presented here. The unselfish guidance he provided me is outdone only by the remarkable insight he holds into the operation of the Sri Lankan political system and the written command of the English language. I owe him a great debt of thanks for his contribution.

Others to whom I am forever indebted include A. Jeyaratnam Wilson of the University of New Brunswick for his invaluable comments on the final version of this manuscript, Ronald H. McDonald, Susan S. Wadley, Linda Fowler, and John Hodgson all of Syracuse University, and Alwyn Rouyer of the University of Idaho who gave me the original drive and desire to tackle a project of this nature. I also owe special thanks to the Nebraska Wesleyan University Faculty Development Fund for its financial contribution to assist the final preparation of this manuscript. Finally, I would like to thank Beverlye Neth who had to put up with my errors and idiosyncracies while typing the final version of the manuscript and Jeanne Hartford who provided last minute help.

                                               Robert Oberst

1
Introduction

This is a study of representation and the role that it plays in a Third World democracy. It explores the nature of the relationship between legislators and their constituents in the South Asian democracy of Sri Lanka.[1] Research to date on representation has not led to a clear and concise understanding of what representation is. In fact, one scholar has described representation as "an ill-defined concept that has acquired conflicting meanings through long use" (Lowenberg, 1972:12). Another, Heinz Eulau (1978:32), has stated that "there is a crisis in the theory of representation." He added that "our colleagues in the field of comparative politics do not deal with it in the familiar terms because they do not find our inherited formulations of representation particularly germane to the real-world problems with which the new nation builders must deal" (Eulau, 1978:32).[2]

This study will explore the applicability of these "inherited formulations of representation" in the context of a modernizing nation. Sri Lanka provides a unique opportunity to study representation. It has had a history of stable democratic governments since receiving independence in 1948. This stability has been set in an environment of a competitive party system, severe economic problems, and a tense confrontation between the island's two main ethnic groups. In spite of these problems, democracy and political stability have prevailed over the last thirty years. This study will examine the role the Sri Lankan Parliament has played in this stability. It has been argued that legislatures in Third World countries help to legitimize the government and integrate the citizens into a nation-state (Mezey, 1979). It would appear that if the linkages between the Sri Lankan legislators and their constituents are strong, it is possible that this has played an important role in maintaining the political stability and democratic processes that Sri Lankans have become accustomed to. Much of the literature on political stability has stressed the need for popular participation or input into the political system. A basic tenet of Huntington's thesis (1968) in the 1960s was that too much participation could be a negative factor as far as political stability was concerned. It is possible that a strong linkage between the government and the population in modernizing societies may offset the instability that Huntington argued would follow rapid increases in participation. Thus the representational role of the Sri Lankan legislator may have contributed to the political stability that has existed in Sri Lanka since receiving its independence in 1948.

It is in the light of these two concerns, the concept of representation and the political stability of Sri Lanka, that this study was carried out. The remainder of this chapter will describe the context that chapters 3 through 9 are placed in.

Heinz Eulau (1978:32) states "that the recent literature on the politics of the developing nations very rarely uses the concept of representation as an explicitly analytical tool." Perhaps the relatively narrow application of the concept as it has been applied to research on the United States Congress has resulted in its failure to be used elsewhere. If one looks beyond this narrow application, research on representation in the Third World can be found (see Ong, 1976; Chee, 1976; Goodman, 1974; Mezey, 1972). Because this research did not fit into the conceptualization and theory of the researchers on the United States, it has been largely ignored. On South Asia alone there have been several studies dealing with representation (Bailey, 1960; Maheshwari, 1976; Mohapatra, 1976). However, these studies are not bound by broader theoretical approaches and are not readily applicable or comparable to other systems. Yet, they reflect the reality of the representational relationship as it exists in South Asia more accurately than conceptual frameworks derived from research in the United States.[3]

Gerhard Loewenberg has noted (1972:12) that the conceptual framework derived from research on the United States Congress has produced a confusing body of findings. It will be argued that some of this confusion has arisen because of the focus of this research on the roll call behavior of United States Congressmen and women and the equation of this behavior with representation. Recent research has changed this focus without significantly altering the conceptual framework in which representation research occurs (Fenno, 1978; Eulau and Karps, 1977; Fiorina, 1977). This research has broadened the definition of what constitutes representation but has failed to change any of the conceptual constructs that are used to study representation. The following section makes six observations concerning representation that are based on the research to date. Each of these observations has relevance to the Sri Lankan situation and the focus of this study. The observations will summarize recent findings in the study of representation and apply them to this study.

(1) The first point concerns the definition of representation. The early studies of representation presented a very narrow view of representational behavior (Turner, 1951; Eulau et al., 1962; MacRae, 1958). This view confined representational behavior to the congruence between a legislator's policy choices and the policy desires of his constituents. This view was prevalent in the representation studies done in the United States until the mid-1970s when Eulau and Karps (1977) expanded the conceptualization of representation to include three additional components of a representative's job.[4] These additional components are constituency service, or the granting of benefits which are highly personalized; the delivery of public goods such as public works and development projects; and symbolic acts of importance to constituents. At the time of their article, a large body of literature on Africa and Asia existed which studied these additional components (Boynton and Kim, 1974). Boynton and Kim have argued that many legislators outside the United States are relatively ineffective in exercising policy influence. In fact, Loewenberg and Patterson (1979:43) argue that when one examines the legislatures of other countries, law-making is not found to be the most important function of the legislatures. They note that John Stuart Mill argued "that a representative assembly was 'radically unfit' for the 'function of governing' but ideal as 'the nation's Committee of Grievances, and its Congress of Opinion.'" Thus, these legislatures do not adequately fit into research frameworks which stress policy congruence.

This study will focus on three components of a legislator's job: law-making, constituency service, and the use of government funds for development and public works projects.[5] It is expected that the representational relationship will vary among the different components of the job.

(2) A second point about representation is that legislators have an orientation to or an attitude about their job. Eulau and associates (1959) described these orientations in their early use of role theory to explain whether legislators make their roll call choices based on their constituent's party or personal preferences. A later scholar (Mezey, 1979:170) has described role orientations as the perceptions of the legislators about what they should be doing. The original role categories suggested by Eulau and associates (1959; also

see Eulau, 1962) have played an important part in the research that followed their work. However, these categories have come under recent criticism. It has been argued that the original role categories were useful for the purposes of their study "but have proved to be less relevant to some types of legislatures than to others" (Mezey, 1979:170). Eulau was "interested in the extent to which legislators felt bound by the views of their constituents when they were deciding upon public policies" (Mezey, 1979:171) The use of their three representational roles--delegate, trustee, and politico--fit the emphasis in their research on policy congruence. As noted earlier, a legislator's job has additional components, and in one component the legislator may represent constituent interests, while in others he may make an individual judgment, or act for his party. Classifying legislators into separate representational role categories may obscure variations in their actions in different components of the job. Thus, the use of role theory may not be applicable to the broadened conceptualization of representation suggested by Eulau and Karps.

(3) A third point concerns the expectations of the "mass and elite public," which Michael Mezey (1978:170) describes as "demands." Demands are the requests that the public makes of legislators. To adequately explore this aspect of the relationship, it would be necessary to carry out survey research among the constituents in a political system (Eulau and Karps, 1978:229). Very little of the research on representation has looked at the attitudes of the public (Jewell, 1983:317; see Kim et al., 1983). An early and highly influential study by Donald Stokes and Warren Miller (1963) did examine constituent's beliefs and knowledge regarding the policies of their legislators. However, this study used a relatively small sample of constituents for each legislator and the concept of representation was confined to the congruence between legislators and constituents on policy options. Eulau and Karps (1977:233) have noted that Stokes and Miller's innovative approach was later "vulgarized" by researchers who equated congruence between legislators and constituents on policy matters to representation. Stokes and Miller, along with most of the later research, concluded that constituents had limited influence on their legislators (Shannon, 1968, Claussen, 1973). This may have resulted in researchers negating the effects of the constituent's demands on legislators. Recent research has led to a refocusing of the effects that constituents may have on their legislators. Fenno (1978), in particular, has noted the interaction that exists between the members of the United States Congress and their constituents outside the realm of law and policy making.

The present study examines constituent demands

placed on Sri Lankan legislators from the perspective of the legislators. This, of course, presents a one-sided view of the demands but, without additional data, it provides an opportunity to analyze the interactions between legislators and their constituents. The demands of the constituents are dealt with in Chapter 4. It is expected that the nature of demands will vary between the different components of the job.

(4) The fourth factor follows directly from the previous three. Legislators and constituents are engaged in a highly interactive and dynamic relationship. The earlier confinement of representational behavior to policy options narrowed the focus of the representational relationship. Legislators were not seen as interacting with their constituents. The nature of the relationship between legislators and constituents was viewed as more or less static (Wahlke, 1975:13), with legislators deciding on the specific role they would follow in the legislature and carrying out that role, behaving as the role dictated. Many have argued that the relationship between legislators and their constituents was weak (MacRae, 1952; Shannon, 1968) or indirect (Pitkin, 1968). Thus, the research focused on the representative and ignored the interaction between the two parties to the relationship.

Recent research on the United States has indicated that the relationship is far more complex than originally believed and that the members of the United States Congress and their constituents interact far more extensively than was originally thought (Fenno, 1978). It is this dynamic interactive process that is conceptualized in this study. Legislators are made aware of the needs of the public and respond to them in some way. The public will make its needs known to the legislators and has the ability to punish the legislator. That which the constituents present to their legislator shapes the nature of the responses that the legislator makes. Fenno (1978:241) has noted that in the eyes of the members of the United States Congress, two-way communication is more valued by their constituents than policy congruence." It is this communication that will be measured by the frequency and content of meetings by the Sri Lankan legislators with the public, along with the legislator's response to the public's demands.

(5) A fifth point deals with a subject that has been largely ignored by the role theorists in their research on representation. This is the structure of the institution and the effects that this structure has on the representational behavior of the legislators. George H. Mead (1956:261), an early "role" theorist, has stated that "in the community, there are certain ways of acting under situations which are essentially identical, and these ways of action on the part of anyone are those which we excite in others when we take

certain steps." Individuals make common responses in similar situations.

> The individual possesses a self only in relation to the selves of the other members of his social group; and the structure of his self expresses or reflects the general behavior pattern of this social group to which he belongs, just as does the structure of the self of every other individual belonging to this social group (Mead, 1956:241).

The belief that an individual acts not only in his own perspective but also in the perspective of a group has significance to understanding the behavior of legislators. A later writer has argued that:

> organizational influence upon the individual may then be interpreted not as determination by the organization of the decisions of the individual, but as determination for him of some of the premises upon which his decisions are based (Simon, 1961:123).

> It is impossible for the behavior of a single isolated individual to reach any high degree of rationality...Individual choice takes place in an environment of "givens"--premises that are accepted by the subject as the basis for his choice; and behavior is adaptive only within the limits set by these "givens" (Simon, 1961:79).

The "givens" of an institution, such as a legislature, help to determine the behavior of the actors in the institution.

Herbert Simon (1961:102-3) has argued that organizations have certain mechanisms which direct the behavior of the actors. These mechanisms can be applied to legislatures. They are: (1) "The organization divides work among its members. By giving each a particular task to accomplish, it directs and limits his attention to that task" (2) It sets certain standards on how certain tasks should be performed; (3) "The organization transmits decisions downward (and laterally or even upward) through its ranks by establishing systems of authority and influence;" (4) "The organization trains and indoctrinates its members...The organization member acquires knowledge, skill, and identifications or loyalties that enable him to make decisions by himself, as the organization would like him to decide."

These mechanisms may direct the legislators into certain patterns of behavior which affect the way in which they represent their constituents. It is argued that these mechanisms have a strong influence on the nature and content of a Sri Lankan MP's job and as a result of this have a significant impact on the representational relationship between the constituents and their legislators. Individual choice plays a part in how legislators perceive their job but other forces are at work which direct their behavior. These forces are the electoral system used to elect legislators; the structure of the institution; and the formal authority one holds in the parliament, such as a ministership. The legislator is not forced to make a decision on how he will act but finds that certain behavior is not possible if one is a minister, or if one is a backbencher.[6] These constraints on the behavior of the legislator are discussed more fully in Chapters 3 through 7.

(6) Related to the structure of the legislature is the nature of the electoral system under which the legislators have been elected. Other writers have described the impact of the single-member electoral constituency and proportional representation on political systems (Rae 1968; Oberst 1984). Few however have acknowledged the impact that the electoral formulae may have on legislative behavior in a political system and on the nature of demands placed on the legislators by their constituents. The structure of the electoral system may direct the legislators and their constituents into certain patterns of behavior which affect the way in which they relate to each other. It is argued that these electoral mechanisms have a strong influence on the nature of representation in Sri Lanka. The single-member electoral constituencies that were used in Sri Lanka to elect the members of parliament studied in this book have helped to create the current representational relationship between the legislators and their constituents.[7]

The following chapters explain the interaction between the legislators and constituents of Sri Lanka in more detail. They argue that representation in Sri Lanka is similar in some respects to representation in the United States and other Western democracies. This is despite the parliamentary context in which the representational relationship occurs in Sri Lanka. Among the major differences are the union of the executive and legislative branches of government.[8] In Sri Lanka, the cabinet ministers carry out all executive functions of government. The cabinet of ministers is made up of the legislative leaders of the dominant party or coalition in the legislature.[9] This leads to a legislature that largely acts to ratify the cabinet's decisions. In Sri Lanka a strong tradition of party loyalty dictates that party members follow party decisions about how to vote on roll calls or risk expulsion from the party.[10] This effectively limits the importance of the law-making component of the legislator's job since the legislator is not free to vote as he sees fit to vote.

The literature on United States legislators has stressed the law-making component of the job because of the greater significance of roll call votes in the United States Congress. As a result, Sri Lanka offers an opportunity to study a system (parliamentary) in which a legislator's job is not dominated by the law-making component of the job because the individual legislator has little input into law-making. If law-making is an important part of representation as many earlier researchers thought it to be, how does representation occur when legislators do not have individual input into this component of their work? Of course it can be argued that Pitkin's thesis (1968) about the indirect nature of representation is accurate in this situation. Yet in the other components of the job, it would appear that legislators make individual decisions and are evaluated individually and not collectively. This point is resolved in Chapter 8 of this study.

Although differences exist between parliamentary and presidential systems, and between industrialized and Third World nations, representation is believed to have many elements common to both. The failure of Third World researchers to use the concepts generated in the research on United States legislators is not a result of the differences between the two systems but rather a failure of the researchers studying the United States Congress to accurately perceive the nature of representation. As noted in the points discussed earlier, several basic tenets of representation theory not only fail to fit a Third World nation such as Sri Lanka but are too limited to explain legislative behavior in the United States. This is largely the result of the United States researchers' preoccupation with law-making at the exclusion of constituency service and development work. Merely noting that there are additional components of legislator's jobs as Eulau and Karps (1977) do is not enough. It is argued here that the expansion of the conceptualization of representation has also created a need to change several of the basic assumptions about representation that had been developed from the literature using the narrower definition of the concept.

This study will argue that representation is a fundamentally different concept than the earlier researchers believed it to be. Representation as it occurs in constituency service and development work is an interactive process, part of an ongoing relationship between legislators and their constituents. It is marked by constituent demands on the legislator, and legislator responses to these demands. In addition, legislators have a desire to satisfy nearly every demand with their only limitation being the resources available to them. The nature of most decisions made by the legislators are noncontroversial and a decision to satisfy one constituent's or group of constituents' demands is not necessarily a refusal to satisy any other demands. Thus, legislators "appropriate all the public credit generated in the system" of demands while others absorb the costs and faults of the system such as the blame for the failure to satisfy all needs (Fiorina, 1977:71). This stress on constituency service and development work provides a linkage between the voters and their government which helps to create a sense of political efficacy in the voters, and provide an outlet for dissatisfaction among the nation's population.

The following chapters elaborate on this argument and present evidence supporting it. Chapter 2 describes the study, and the political and social environment in which it occurred. Chapter 3 examines the legislators' attitudes about their job and what they see as important. Evidence is presented which shows the low stature of law-making and the importance of constituency demands on the legislators. Here, evidence is reported which shows that the constituents do not make many demands concerning law-making to their legislators. In addition, it is argued that the culture and traditions of Sri Lanka have helped to shape the nature of the legislators' representational responses and the constituents' demands. Chapters 5, 6, and 7 describe how the representational relationship operates in the three components of a legislator's job in Sri Lanka; constituency service, law-making and development work. These chapters note the lack of input most members have into national policy and legislation, and focus on their extensive interactions in constituency service and development work. Chapter 8 summarizes the findings and attempts to present a model of how representation operates in Sri Lanka while Chapter 9 discusses the theoretical implications of the study.

NOTES

1. Prior to 1972, Sri Lanka was called by the British name of Ceylon. All references to the country will use the name of Sri Lanka.

2. Eulau does note that Lucien Pye (1966:21, 24-26) deals with the question of representation "in its own terms." Pye's use of representation resembles the conceptualization of it dominant at that time in the United States with which Eulau was, of course, quite comfortable.

3. For instance, Weinbaum (1957:34) argues that role analysis is culturally bound.

4. Although Eulau and Karp's conceptualization has largely been accepted by other scholars some continue to equate

representation with policy congruence. Once study (Alpert, 1979:587) limits role theory to policy preferences. "The representational role is an analytical concept that describes the behavioral orientation of a legislator toward the policy preferences of his constituency."

5. The fourth component suggested by Eulau and Karps (1977), that of symbolic actions, is not included in this analysis. It was felt that symbolic goods were a part of each of the other components of a legislator's job and therefore the examination of them separately would be repetitious.

6. A backbencher is a well known term used in parliaments. Ministers and deputy ministers occupy the front rows or benches of the parliament. All other members sit in the "back benches." Thus, the term backbencher is commonly used to describe those government MPs who hold no formal authority in the parliament.

7. The Constitution of 1978 abolished the single-member electoral constituency. However, no national elections have been held yet using proportional representation. The next parliamentary elections are not expected until 1988.

8. The Constitution of 1978 (discussed in Chapter 2) created a presidential-parliamentary system similar to that of France. However, this change did not alter the union of legislature and executive.

9. Throughout this study, the cabinet of ministers will be treated as a part of the legislature. As will become apparent in later chapters, cabinet ministers are a privileged elite in the legislature and are set apart from the rest of the members on the basis of their power and behavior.

10. The Constitution of 1978 effectively gives the political party control over parliamentary seats. The party has the power to expel any member from parliament who was elected on the party label. This guarantees party loyalty on roll call votes. The second amendment to the constitution gives the governing party the power to determine whether opposition parties may expel their members during the first parliament under the constitution.

2
Sri Lankan Society and Politics

      The research for this study was carried out from August 1978 to July 1979. It involved interviews with 102 members and ex-members of the Sri Lankan Parliament. All but five of those interviewed had been or were members of the Seventh and Eighth Parliaments of Sri Lanka.[1] The term of the Seventh Parliament lasted from June 1970 to July 1977. The Eighth Parliament first sat in July 1977 and has continued to sit until the present time.[2] Selection of respondents was non-random but was stratified to include both a broad ethnic and geographic distribution of members.[3] The length of the interviews averaged about an hour and fifteen minutes with the shortest lasting about thirty minutes and several running well over three hours. The questions asked in the interviews followed no particular order except that all members were asked to discuss certain topics which dealt with areas where data was sought. Notes were taken during the interviews and rewritten later. Appendix A lists the topics discussed in the interviews and the data sought under each topic.
      Other researchers of Sri Lankan politics have been criticised for focusing too heavily on the leaders who reside in Colombo and for tending to ignore the large numbers of MPs who reside in the rural areas of the country. It is argued that those leaders residing in Colombo are not representative of the large rural segment of the population of the country. This study focuses very heavily on these rural MPs and tends to underrepresent the MPs residing in Colombo.[4] A majority of the interviews occurred in the electorates of the members involved.
      Table 2.1 reports the geographic distribution by province of the MPs interviewed and the number of seats from that province in the Eighth Parliament. Table 2.2 reports the party affiliation of those interviewed and the support those parties had in the Seventh and Eighth Parliaments. The geographic distribution of the MPs interviewed roughly approximates the actual distribution

TABLE 2.1
Distribution of members interviewed by province

	Number Interviewed	Percent of Total Interviewed	Seats in Eighth Parliament	Percent of Total Seats
Western	15	14.9	39	23.2
Central	19	18.8	24	14.3
Southern	14	13.9	21	12.5
Northwestern	14	13.9	19	11.3
Northcentral	3	3.0	10	6.0
Northern	11	10.9	14	8.3
Eastern	12	11.9	12	7.1
Uva	5	5.0	12	7.1
Sabaragamuva	8	7.9	17	10.1

Note: Total equals 101 members interviewed because one interviewee was an appointed member and thus, represented no province.

TABLE 2.2
Distribution of MPs interviewed by party

	Number Interviewed	Percent of Total Interviewed	Seats in 7th & 8th Parliaments[a]	Percent of Total Seats
United National Party	32	33.0	150	49.8
Sri Lanka Freedom Party	35	36.1	97	32.2
Lanka Sama Samaja Party	8	8.2	19	6.3
Communist Party	4	4.1	6	2.0
Tamil parties[b]	16	16.5	27	9.0
Independents	2	2.0	3	1.0

[a] The number of seats held by a party in the Seventh and Eighth Parliaments is the number of party members who were in parliament. Thus, if a party member sat in both parliaments, he or she is counted only once.

[b] The Tamil parties are the Federal Party, Tamil Congress, Tamil United Liberation Front and the Ceylon Workers Congress.

among all members of parliament. The party distribution tends to favor the smaller parties and the Sri Lanka Freedom Party at the expense of the United National Party. This is, in part, the result of the large numbers of United National Party members in the Eighth Parliament (see Table 2.5). The two major parties, the United National Party and the Sri Lanka Freedom Party, are about equal in total numbers of MPs interviewed. The sample bias in favor of the smaller parties also skews the sample in favor of the Tamil ethnic group.[5] (The ethnic groups of Sri Lanka will be described later in this chapter.) A conscious attempt was made to include members of ethnic minorities in the sample and thus, such groups as the Tamils, the Moors, low caste groups, and Burghers are overrepresented.

SOCIAL AND POLITICAL SETTING

Sri Lanka is a small pearl shaped island in the Indian Ocean at the foot of the South Asian subcontinent. It is 25,332 square miles in area or about the size of the United States' state of Massachusetts. Its population is about 15 million people, making it one of the most densely populated countries in the world. During the 1950s, Sri Lanka had one of the highest population growth rates in the world at 3.1 percent a year (Abayasekera, 1976:10). Successful family planning measures have led to a decline in the growth rate to below 2 percent a year, one of the lowest rates in Asia.

Sri Lanka received its political independence from Great Britain in 1948 after four centuries of colonial rule that began with the Portuguese, who were followed by the Dutch and finally the British in 1796. The colonial powers were unable to gain control of the rugged mountainous interior of Sri Lanka until the British subdued and conquered the Kandyan Kingdom in 1815. As a result of its long independence from colonial domination, the people of the hill country of Sri Lanka maintained attachments to indigenous forms of government and social behavior that persisted even after the British takeover.

Sri Lanka is marked by a great deal of ethnic diversity. The largest ethnic group on the island is the Sinhalese (see Table 2.3). The Sinhalese claim they are descendants of early settlers from North India.[6] They speak an Indo-Aryan language, Sinhala, which is related to the languages of North India and are the only people in the world to speak this language. This has led to a strong sense of ethnic identity among the Sinhalese. They feel that they must protect themselves from the cultural influences of the numerically larger Tamil culture of South India. Representatives of this culture live in Sri Lanka and are called either Sri Lanka or

TABLE 2.3
Ethnic population of Sri Lanka

Ethnic Group	Percent of Population	Percent of Members of Eighth Parliament
Sinhalese	74.0	81.0
Ceylon Tamils	12.6	11.3
Indian Tamils	5.6	.6
Ceylon Moors	7.1	7.1
Burghers	.3	.0
Malays	.3	.0

Source: <u>Statistical Abstract of the Democratic Socialist Republic of Sri Lanka-1982</u> (Colombo: Department of Census and Statistics, 1983), p. 32.

or Indian Tamils.[7] The Sri Lanka Tamils are descendants of Tamil speaking people who came from South India over one thousand years ago. They continue to speak Tamil which is a Dravidian language and thus related to the languages of Southern India. This sets them apart from the Indo-Aryan Sinhalese both linguistically and culturally.

The Indian Tamils are the descendants of laborers who were brought by British planters from South India in the late nineteenth and early twentieth centuries largely to work on their tea estates in the mountainous interior of Sri Lanka. They speak Tamil, and many feel culturally differentiated from the Sri Lanka Tamils, even though they trace their origins to the same area of India and speak the same language (Devaraj 1984: 162-163). Shortly after independence, the Indian Tamils were denied citizenship and under an agreement with India in 1964, some have been sent to India while others have been granted Sri Lankan citizenship. Implementation of this agreement has been very slow and nearly one hundred thousand continue to remain stateless. However, the number of Indian Tamils receiving Sri Lankan citizenship has been increasing and one of them was elected to parliament in 1977.[8] This was the first time since the 1947 general elections that an Indian Tamil was elected to parliament.

The Sri Lanka Moors are the descendants of Indian and Middle Eastern traders who came to Sri Lanka in medieval times. Almost all of them practice Islam and generally speak Tamil. The Burghers are people of mixed Sri Lankan and European ancestry. Their native tongue is English, and most live in the Colombo[9] area and are highly westernized.

The ethnic identities of these groups are

reinforced not only by their language, which tends to conform to the groups, but by their religion as well. Thus, the Sinhalese speak Sinhala and are mostly Buddhist, while the Tamils speak Tamil and are largely Hindu. The Moors are almost all Muslims and speak Tamil. In addition to these three religions, relatively large numbers of Christians are found among the Sinhalese and Tamils. For a breakdown of religious groups see Table 2.4.

In addition to these divisions, the people of Sri Lanka are divided on the basis of caste. Although the caste structure in Sri Lanka is not as rigid as it is in India, caste still plays an important part in the social and political behavior of the country. The Sinhalese and Tamils have separate and distinct caste structures while the Moors do not make caste distinctions.

There has not been a census enumeration of caste in this century in Sri Lanka (Jiggins 1979:29) and, therefore, no reliable figures on the caste population exist. However, among the Sinhalese, it has been estimated that the Goyigama caste comprises over 50 percent of the Sinhalese population (Ryan, 1951).[10] The Goyigama or cultivator caste is at the top of the status hierarchy of caste among the Sinhalese. They have dominated the governments of independent Sri Lanka and with the exception of the present prime minister, Ranasinghe Premadasa[11], all of the prime ministers of Sri Lanka have come from the Goyigama caste. Just beneath the Goyigama on the status hierarchy are three smaller castes, the Karawa (fishermen), the Salagama (cinnamon peelers), and the Durawa (toddy tappers). These three castes are concentrated along the southwestern coast of the island and exercise extensive influence in that area.

TABLE 2.4
Religious composition of the Sri Lankan population

Religion	Percent of Population
Buddhists	69.3
Hindus	15.5
Muslims	7.6
Christians	7.5
Others	.1

Source: Statistical Abstract, p. 34.

The <u>Wahumpara</u> (jaggery makers) and <u>Batgam</u> (of uncertain occupational origin) castes are two of the more significant castes of relatively low status. Both of these castes are found in the interior hill country in relatively large numbers and have had several representatives in parliament. An important feature of the caste situation in Sri Lanka is their geographic concentration. Unlike India where a village may have representatives of many castes, Sri Lankan villages usually have an overwhelming majority of one caste. In addition, other villages in the vicinity are likely to be populated by the same caste. This provides an opportunity for these smaller castes to gain representation in parliament since electoral districts can be constructed in which they comprise a majority of the population. Several electoral districts have been created specifically to give representation to these minorities.

Among the Sri Lanka Tamils, the <u>Vellala</u> (cultivators) caste has a similar position to that of the Goyigama among the Sinhalese. They have been socially, economically and politically dominant in the Sri Lanka Tamil society (Pfaffenberger 1982:38-42).[12] The <u>Koviyar</u> (domestic servants) caste stands next to the Vellala in status. Two fishing castes, the <u>Karayar</u> found along the northern coast and the <u>Mukkuvar</u> found along the east coast are also of significant size. Among the Sri Lanka Tamils there are four "untouchable" castes. These are the <u>Palla</u> (agricultural laborers), the <u>Nalava</u> (toddy tappers), the <u>Ambattar</u> (barbers) and the <u>Paraya</u> (scavengers). In the Eighth General Elections of 1977, a member of one of the untouchable castes, the Palla caste, was elected to parliament. It was the first time an untouchable had been elected to the Sri Lankan parliament.[13] Most of the Tamil MPs have come from the Vellala caste. This has been especially the case with the leadership of the Tamil political parties. (These parties will be discussed later in this chapter).

It is within this ethnic diversity that Great Britain established a political system based on the British system. They left a heritage of democratic parliamentary government based on the Westminster model of government. The parliament of independent Sri Lanka has been structured by three constitutions. The first of these was the Soulbury Constitution of 1946 which established a bicameral legislature with a lower chamber called the House of Representatives and an upper chamber called the Senate. This was replaced by a new constitution with a unicameral legislature in 1972 which in turn was replaced six years later after the opposition party took power in 1977. The new constitution of 1978 established a modified presidential system retaining the unicameral parliament and president but placing many of the powers of the prime minister in the hands of the president.

The parliament sits continuously throughout the year, holding two meetings a month unless business necessitates more. During the annual debate on the budget, parliament sits continuously for about a month. The parliament has traditionally been dominated by the cabinet. Prior to the Constitution of 1978 it was selected by the prime minister. Since 1978 the president has selected the cabinet in consultation with the prime minister.

Under the provisions of the Soulbury Constitution, the prime minister was allowed to select a certain number of members of parliament to represent groups which were not "adequately" represented in the parliament. In 1970, at the beginning of the Seventh Parliament, six non-elected members were selected in this way. The Constitution of 1972 abandoned this practice but allowed those members appointed in 1970 to remain in parliament until the term of parliament ended. All other members are elected directly to parliament.[14] Most of these are elected in single-member electoral constituencies although in the 1970 general elections five out of 145 electorates returned two or three members from multi-member constituencies, while in the 1977 general elections six out of 160 electorates returned two or three members from multi-member electorates.

The cabinet is the focus of the policy making process in Sri Lanka. Its size has been increasing in recent parliaments and in a cabinet change in February 1980 the number of ministries was increased to thirty-five. Each ministry may be assisted by a junior minister commonly called a deputy minister.[15] Their functions are defined by the minister of their ministry and, thus, the power exerted by each deputy minister varies from ministry to ministry. In addition, they may serve as acting minister if the minister leaves the country or is indisposed.

In the Eighth Parliament, the post of district minister was created. This position exists for each of the twenty-four administrative districts on the island. The district ministers oversee the administration of government development projects in their districts and the work of the departments doing the projects. In addition, the district minister dominates the executive committee of the District Development Councils (DDC) created in 1981. The district minister's position on the DDCs corresponds to that of the president at the national level of government (Matthews 1982:1121).

As already noted, Sri Lanka is divided into twenty-four administrative districts.[16] In each district, the administration of government is overseen by the government agent who became the permanent secretary to the district minister with the advent of the district ministry scheme in 1978. The government agents exercise a great deal of influence over the governmental administration in their districts although most of the departments in the districts also have vertical lines of authority to their central offices in Colombo. Beneath the district level of government, there is a myriad of government bodies at the municipal, urban, town and village level. The members of these bodies are elected and the position is often used as a starting point for a career in parliament.

In the first two elections after independence, 1947 and 1952, the United National Party (UNP) easily became the dominant political party in the country. The party was a broadly based coalition of ideological moderates who had participated in the independence movement during the British era. They were challenged in the elections by two Marxist parties, the Lanka Sama Samaja Party (LSSP), a Trotskyite party, and the Communist Party of Ceylon (CP). The UNP received the support of many ideological rightists and acquired the image of being the party of the right. In 1952, one of the founders of the UNP, Solomon West Ridgeway Dias Bandaranaike, split with the party and formed the Sri Lanka Freedom Party (SLFP). His new party championed the interests of the rural peasantry and attempted to provide the voters with an alternative to the Marxists and the rightists.

In 1956, Bandaranaike was able to put together a coalition of anti-UNP and leftist forces and defeat the UNP at the polls. Bandaranaike was assassinated in 1959 and his coalition separated into a large number of small parties, each one organized around its own charismatic leader. What was left of the SLFP lost the March, 1960 general elections to the UNP. The UNP was unable to obtain the support of a majority of parliament and new elections were called for July, 1960. In these elections the SLFP, now led by S.W.R.D. Bandaranaike's widow, Sirimavo, won with a narrow majority. The party entered into a short lived coalition with the LSSP in 1964 before the 1965 elections. The 1965 general elections were won by the UNP, which ruled until 1970. In 1970, the SLFP went into a coalition with the CP and LSSP, and won the election easily. (See Table 2.5 for a breakdown of the election results.) In 1975, the LSSP was forced out of the coalition and in 1977, shortly before the general elections of that year, the CP left the coalition. The 1977 general elections were won easily by the UNP as the three former coalition partners contested the election by themselves (see Table 2.5).

In October 1982, the first presidential election under the 1978 constitution was held. It was won by the incumbent Junius Richard Jayawardene. Jayawardene had been appointed to the post shortly before the promulgation of the new constitution with the argument that he did not need to be elected because of his selection by

TABLE 2.5
Party positions following the elections of 1970 and 1977

	1970 Seats Won	1977 Seats Won
SLFP	91	8
UNP	17	140
LSSP	19	0
CP	6	0
FP	13	---
TC	3	---
TULF	---	18
APPOINTED MPs	6	---
INDEPENDENTS	2	1
TOTAL	157	167

parliament as prime minister (Wilson 1980:7). In December of 1982, a referendum was held.[17] It offered the voters the opportunity of continuing the current parliament for six more years. A majority of the voters (54.5 percent) supported the proposition and the parliament elected in 1977 was extended until 1989.[18]

In addition to these four parties, two parties with support among the Sri Lanka Tamils have been of importance. These parties, the Federal Party (FP) and the Tamil Congress (TC) united in the early 1970s to form the Tamil United Liberation Front (TULF). These parties have had strong support among the Sri Lanka Tamils in the Northern and Eastern parts of the island--areas dominated by that ethnic group. The TULF, and Federal Party before it, have advocated very strong positions for either autonomy or independence for the Tamil areas of the country. During the Seventh Parliament the FP was in opposition to the SLFP coalition while two of the three parliamentary members of the Tamil Congress and one Federal Party member joined the governing coalition. In the Eighth Parliament, the TULF was the largest opposition party in parliament and led the opposition to the UNP until 1983. In the summer of 1983, the Sixth Amendment to the constitution banned the promotion of separatist sentiments. On October 22, 1983, eleven members of the TULF refused to pledge an oath disavowing separatist beliefs and were expelled from parliament. Consequently the SLFP became the major party in opposition and its leader became the leader of the opposition because it now had the largest representation of members in parliament.

Thus, the Sri Lankan party system has developed

into a highly competitive system with several parties, although only the UNP and the SLFP have enough electoral support to win a majority in parliament on their own. Political debate between the parties has centered on two main themes. The first is the role that the government should take in the economy. The SLFP and its Marxist allies have argued for strict economic controls over the private sector, an extensive social welfare system, and direct government involvement over the means of production. The UNP has supported a free market system with a limited role by the government. While in power they have usually curtailed the extent of social welfare benefits and reduced the number of economic controls and productive enterprises run by the government.

The second theme involves the ethnic differences between the Tamils and Sinhalese. At the time of independence the language of government was English, a language in which the Tamils were, in general, more proficient than the Sinhalese. In 1956, after the SLFP victory, the government acted to increase the role of the Sinhalese ethnic group in both the commercial and governmental life of the society. Their first legislative enactment made Sinhala the language of government. The UNP quickly accepted this idea in principle. Since that time, the Tamils have increasingly felt isolated and excluded from the Sinhalese society and government. In order to protect their interests they have demanded more autonomy for the Tamil speaking areas of the country. In recent years, these demands have led to calls for an independent Tamil nation. These calls have been accompanied by a guerilla movement led by Tamil youths and a series of communal riots directed against the Tamils in 1977, 1981 and 1983.

It is within this environment of strong allegiances to ethnic attachments and a highly competitive party system that this study of representation and the linkages between the legislators and their constituents was made. The next chapter describes the Sri Lankan legislators' attitudes about their job and how they spend their time.

NOTES

1. Despite the promulgation of a new constitution in 1978 which drastically altered the Sri Lankan political system all but one of the respondents in this survey were elected under similar electoral conditions. In addition, despite the 1978 constitution's abolition of the single-member electoral constituency (in favor of a system of proportional representation) there was little apparent change in the attitudes and behavior of the Eighth Parliament MPs toward the electorates they were elected to parliament from under the old constitution.

2. The Sri Lankan electorate voted in support of a proposition extending the life of parliament for an additional six years in a referendum held in December 1982.

3. An attempt was made to interview a random sample. This failed due to several ex-members living outside the country and an inability to contact several other members.

4. As will be brought out later, much of the interaction between legislators and constituents occurs between backbenchers and their constituents. The MPs residing in Colombo were more likely to be ministers and as a result were undersampled.

5. This was done to obtain some indication of what attitudes the members of the minority ethnic groups and parties held. As will be noted later in this chapter, the minority ethnic groups are a significant part of Sri Lankan politics. Thus they were oversampled in order to obtain a large enough sample with which to examine their beliefs.

6. The term Sinhalese will be used to describe the ethnic group while the term Sinhala will be used to describe the language the Sinhalese speak.

7. Since the name change of Ceylon to Sri Lanka, the term Sri Lanka Tamils has begun to be used to describe this ethnic group rather than the earlier term Ceylon Tamil still used in the Statistical Abstract of Sri Lanka (see Table 2.3).

8. Sauvmiamoorthy Thondaman was elected to parliament from the three-member constituency of Nuwara Eliya-Maskeliya in the 1977 general elections. Earlier he had also been elected a member of the First Parliament from 1947 to 1952. In 1977 he was elected as a member of the Ceylon Workers Congress, which is the political wing of the largest union in Sri Lanka.

9. Colombo is the capital city of Sri Lanka. It is located on the southwestern coast in the heart of the Sinhalese area of the country, although its population includes large numbers of Tamils and Moors.

10. Jiggins (1979:34-35) estimates that 56.2 percent of the Sinhalese belong to the Goyigama caste.

11. The Constitution of 1978 transferred many of the powers of the prime minister to the president. Thus, Premadasa does not hold the power that earlier prime ministers have held. That power is held by the president, who happens to be a member of the Goyigama caste.

12. Pfaffenberger (1984:47) estimates that the Vellala comprise 50 percent of the Jaffna Tamil population.

13. An untouchable had been appointed to the Seventh Parliament under the provisions for appointed members in the Soulbury Constitution. He was a Communist Party member from Jaffna.

14. The Constitution of 1978 provides for the election of members of parliament by a system of proportional representation. No members have been selected in this manner and none are expected until the next general election scheduled for 1988.

15. Prior to 1972, deputy ministers were officially called parliamentary secretaries.

16. In 1978, two districts were split in half, creating two new districts and raising the number of districts to twenty-four. In addition to the districts, the island is divided into nine

provinces containing two to three districts each.

17. The Constitution of 1978 provides for a referendum to be held on any bill the cabinet certifies to be submitted as a referendum, or which the Supreme Court determines requires a referendum (Chapter XIII).

18. The election was accompanied by widespread allegations of fraud (Wiswa Warnapala and Hewagama 1983: Chapter VIII).

3
Legislative Attitudes

It is necessary to examine the attitudes of the legislators toward their jobs in parliament in order to understand the nature of the dimensions of their job and to examine the nature of the interactive relationship between the MPs and their constituents. This chapter argues that legislators in Sri Lanka do not "choose" the type of legislator they will be, as has been argued about legislators in the United States (Davidson, 1969:188-89; Jewell and Loewenberg, 1979: 485). Instead, Sri Lankan legislators find that the formal distribution of authority in the parliament structures the work that they do in parliament and strongly affects their attitudes about their jobs. Despite this structuring of the attitudes and jobs of the legislators, they still focus their activities toward their constituencies and many consider this to be important. This is a necessary part of an interactive relationship between the legislators and their constituents.

In addition, it is argued that most legislators are not involved with national issues or policy and do not believe them to be important. This is an indication that representation in Sri Lanka has two dimensions, one of national issues and a second concerning constituency interests.

As is noted in Chapter 1, representation involves a two-way relationship between a legislator and his constituents (Fenno, 1978:237). It is an interaction in which each party to the relationship attempts to affect the behavior of the other party (Zeigler and Baer, 1969:9-11). In a relationship of this nature, the attitudes of the parties involved in it play an important part in its operation (Styskal, 1975:235-236). This chapter examines the attitudes of the Sri Lankan legislators toward the job they are doing and what they believe they should be doing.

In order to gain an idea of what the Sri Lankan members of parliament feel about their job as a legislator, they were asked what they believed to be the most important part of their job as a member of parliament and what aspects of their job consumed the greatest amount of their time.[1] The first part of this question examines what the member believes he should be doing, while the second part indicates what he is doing. The questions were open-ended with no attempt to direct the respondent into certain categories. This, of course, resulted in a wide variety of responses. However, the responses did follow a general trend and a majority of the respondents appeared to base their responses on similar conceptual frameworks.

A problem emerged from the nature of the questions. Even though the questions were open-ended, they still required the respondent to divide the various aspects of the job into isolated parts. There is a great deal of overlap between the various components of their jobs. For example, cabinet ministers' time working in their ministries may be spent dealing either with particularized benefits[2] for their constituents, or preparing legislation for presentation to parliament, or resolving administrative problems in their ministries. In the same sense, time spent by backbenchers in Colombo visiting the office of a minister may involve case work for particularized benefits, the speeding up of development projects in their electorates or in some instances legislation sponsored by the ministry. It is difficult for legislators to isolate these chores in order to provide a researcher with an accurate account of how the legislators' time is spent.

When asked which aspects of their job were the most time consuming, the respondents gave answers which could be placed into four categories. These are: (1) constituency service work or the granting of particularized benefits to one's constituents; (2) the planning and administration of development projects; (3) ministry work, the making of laws and involvement with national issues; and (4) the promotion of one's political party, trade union or ideology.[3]

Constituency service work was cited by over 57 percent of the respondents as the most time consuming part of their job, while over 54 percent of the respondents cited work on development projects as the second most time consuming part of their job. The importance of constituency service work in the use of time by the members is reflected in Table 3.1. Nearly 90 percent of the respondents cited constituency service work as either the first or second most time consuming part of their job, while over 58 percent cited work on development projects as either the most or second most time consuming part of their job.

The responses become more informative when the respondents are separated according to their formal position of authority in parliament. Table 3.2 reports

TABLE 3.1
Time use by MPs in different aspects of job

Type of Work	Most Time Consuming		Second Most Time Consuming	
	no.	percent	no.	percent
Constituency Service	61	57.0	35	33.0
Development Projects	4	3.7	58	54.7
Ministry/Legislation/ National Issues	36	33.6	8	7.5
Party/Trade Unions/ Ideology	6	5.6	5	4.7
Total	107	99.9	106	99.9

Note: Totals in the percent column do not add up to 100 percent due to rounding. The total number of MPs exceeds the number in the sample due to five members providing responses for earlier parliaments as well as the last one they sat in, and one member giving only the most time consuming aspect of his job.

TABLE 3.2
Primary use of time by MPs and formal authority in parliament

Type of Work	Ministers		Deputy Ministers		Back-benchers		Opposition	
	no.	%	no.	%	no.	%	no.	%
Constituency Service	0	0.0	4	20.0	41	93.2	16	64.0
Development Projects	0	0.0	0	0.0	1	2.3	3	12.0
Ministry/Legislation/ National Issues	18	100.0	15	75.0	1	2.3	2	8.0
Party/Trade Unions/ Ideology	0	0.0	1	5.0	1	2.3	4	16.0
Total	18	100.0	20	100.0	44	100.1	25	100.0

Note: The totals in the percent columns do not add up to 100 due to rounding. $X^2=83.7$, significant at the .001 level.

the responses of ministers, deputy ministers, backbenchers and opposition members.[4] A clear pattern can be seen between the ministers and deputy ministers on one hand and the backbenchers and opposition members on the other. The backbench and opposition members spend most of their time dealing with particularized benefits and development projects while the ministers and deputy ministers are occupied with national issues and ministry work, and to a lesser degree particularized benefits.

When asked what aspect of their job as a member of parliament was the most important, the respondents divided approximately evenly between development work[5] and national issues with only about 10 percent citing constituency service or party work (see Table 3.3). Although constituency service work was seen as the most time consuming component of their job, only one member cited it as the most important component. Once again the division between the ministers and deputy ministers, and the backbench and opposition members appears (see Table 3.4) The ministers and deputy ministers overwhelmingly cite ministry work and national issues as the most important part of their jobs while the backbenchers and to a lesser extent, the opposition members cite development projects. The opposition members' concern with national issues reflects their position as the only opposition to the government's policies.

The evidence presented thus far indicates that the way members spend their time and what they consider to be important about their jobs are related to their formal position of authority in parliament. An initial observation would lead to two propositions. The first is that the members' use of time is a function of their

TABLE 3.3
Important aspects of job among all members

Type of Work	Most Important		Second Most Important	
	no.	percent	no.	percent
Constituency Service	1	0.9	36	35.0
Development Projects	45	42.1	46	44.7
Ministry/Legislation/ National Issues	50	46.7	14	13.6
Party/Trade Unions/ Ideology	11	10.3	7	6.8
	107	100.0	103	100.1

Note: Percent totals do not add up to 100 percent due to rounding.

TABLE 3.4
Most important aspect of job and formal authority in parliament

Type of Work	Minister		Deputy Minister		Back-benchers		Opposition	
	no.	%	no.	%	no.	%	no.	%
Constituency Service	0	0.0	1	5.0	1	2.3	0	0.0
Development Projects	1	5.6	1	5.0	32	72.7	10	40.0
Ministry/Legislation/ National Issues	15	83.3	15	75.0	8	18.2	12	48.0
Party/Trade Unions/ Ideology	2	11.1	3	15.0	3	6.8	3	12.0
Total	18	99.9	20	100.0	44	100.0	25	100.0

Note: Totals in the percent columns do not add up to 100 percent due to rounding. $X^2=41.7$, significant at the .001 level.

responsibilities in parliament, as defined by their formal authority, and that this, in turn, affects the demands that the constituents place on them. Their constituents in turn react to their power to respond to demands. The second proposition concerns the attitudes of the legislators about their jobs. Obviously the structure of formal authority in parliament cannot dictate the attitudes of the legislators. It may affect the way they use their time but not how they would like to use it, therefore some legislators will not accept their lack of power over national issues and policy. The Seventh Parliament was marked by a great deal of dissension among the government coalition members. A bloc of backbench legislators belonging to the parties of the government coalition made an active effort to influence and change government policy. As will be noted in Chapter 6, the Sri Lankan backbencher does not have very much influence over policy. This dissension led to several defections from the government coalition during the Seventh Parliament's term of office. It was expected that these defectors might have different attitudes about their jobs. Instead of seeing development work in their electorates as the most important part of their job as do other backbenchers, they might be expected to see national issues as the most important part of their job.

These legislators will be referred to as "rebels" and include eight backbenchers, one minister and one opposition member of the Seventh Parliament, and one deputy minister from the Eighth Parliament. The Eighth Parliament has not been marked by dissension and so far no members can be identified as "rebels" with the exception of the deputy minister mentioned above. The 1978 constitution has restricted the emergence of "rebels." As noted earlier, the constitution allows a political party to remove and replace any of its members in parliament. This inhibits the members from speaking out in opposition to government policies.[6] Table 3.5 reports the use of time and importance of the different aspects of their job among the eight "rebel" backbenchers in the Seventh Parliament. It is apparent that the rebels spend their time in the same way as other backbenchers but appear to resemble the ministers in what they feel is important about their jobs. The rebels were very concerned with national issues and legislation.

All of the rebels attempted to take an active part in the promotion of national issues and legislation. As is noted in Chapter 6, this does not appear to be the function of a backbencher in Sri Lanka. Each one of these members appeared to be rebelling against the accepted distribution of functions in parliament. All but one of the group in the Seventh Parliament were a part of a rebel group in the government's Parliamentary Group that attempted to influence legislation. The small size of this divergent group of legislators may be an indication of the strength of the informal distribution of functions in parliament.

Thus, it would appear that in most cases Sri Lankan legislators do not choose the type of legislator they will be. How they spend their time and what they consider to be important about what they are doing are closely related to the formal authority they hold in parliament. If an MP is given formal authority in the legislature, that authority largely determines the MP's attitudes and behavior about the job. The individual choice of the legislator is stifled by an institutional set of rules and regulations that direct and mold their behavior. Only 3 percent of the backbenchers consider the aspect of their job on which they are spending the largest segment of their time to be the most important part of their work as an MP (see Table 3.6). This compares with 84 percent of the ministers. Very few members have input into the law-making process. This leads to dissatisfaction among those who do not have law-making power and a tendency for them to specialize on that which they are capable of doing.

The remaining chapters of this book examine the three main components of a Sri Lankan MP's job: constituency service, development work, and law-making and examines the members' attitudes toward each aspect. These divisions of labor and the differences between the levels of formal authority in parliament are realities of the job and are perceived by the members as such. Several of the members spoke of a division of labor between the formal positions of authority in the

TABLE 3.5
Use of time and importance of aspects of job among the "rebels"

Type of Work	Time Use		Most Important Aspect of Job	
	number	percent	number	percent
Constituency Service	6	75.0	0	0.0
Development Work	0	0.0	2	25.0
National Issues/ Legislation	2	25.0	6	75.0
Party/Trade Union/ Ideology	0	0.0	0	0.0

TABLE 3.6
Congruence between most important aspect of job and main use of time

	With Main Use of Time		With Secondary or Main Use of Time	
	number	percent	number	percent
Ministers	15	83.3	17	94.4
Deputy Ministers	13	65.0	15	75.0
Backbenchers	1	2.6	28	73.6
Opposition	6	26.1	16	64.0
Rebels	1	12.5	4	50.0

parliament as if they were completely unconnected responsibilities. The term MP is frequently used to refer to a backbencher. One minister who was elevated from backbencher status to his ministry without the intermediate step of being a deputy minister stated that he was glad that he was no longer an MP. "I cease to be an MP. It is much easier to be on top, in the cabinet. A few words and you can shape policy. Parliament is useless for the cabinet minister."[7] A distinction appears to exist between the parliament and the cabinet as if the two were unrelated institutions. Several backbenchers expressed similar sentiments when asked how important law-making was to them. "Backbenchers do not make laws, that is the work of the cabinet."

This chapter has presented an argument that is very important for an understanding of representation in Sri Lanka. First, Sri Lankan MPs appear to have limited power over the way they spend their time as an MP. Second, over one-half of the MPs stated that national issues and law-making were not the most important part of their job. Instead, it appeared that they considered development work to be the most important part of their jobs. Over 84 percent of the MPs stated that development work was either the most or the second most important part of their job. The following chapters bring out the significance of these two points.

The actions of a legislator do not occur in a vaccum. They are influenced by external forces including not only the structure of authority in parliament but pressrues and demands from groups and individuals from within and outside the legislator's constituency. These demands and the relationship that surrounds them are an integral part of representation. The next chapter deals with the nature of constituent demands in Sri Lanka.

NOTES

1. Mezey (1978:171) suggests the use of these questions as a way to find legislative orientations toward their constituents. The use here is much broader, examining all aspects of the job.

2. Particularized benefits will be defined throughout this study as those benefits bestowed by a legislator which benefit a small group of people or a single person and therefore require government actions of a specific nature. "The distinction is not between statutory and nonstatutory responses, but between laws or other government actions with a predominant effect on the individual or group initiating the demand and laws or other actions that have a generalized effect throughout the country" (Mezey, 1978:146).

3. Kearney (1971) argues that trade unions in Sri Lanka are usually adjuncts to political parties, thus they are grouped with party work. In each of the cases of the respondents who cited union work, their union was affiliated with their political party.

4. The position of district minister was created in 1978 during the Eighth Parliament. One district minister was appointed to each of the island's twenty-four administrative districts. They have the authority to oversee development projects in the district. They have been included under the category of deputy ministers. Their salary and staff privileges in parliament are similar to those of the deputy ministers. In addition, they do not appear to have any more prestige or power than do the deputy ministers. Their role is discussed in Chapter 7.

5. A study of state legislators in India has found that the development work role is the most important there (Puri, 1978:247). Also see Narain and Puri (1976:321). Chee (1976) speaks of "linkage" as the most important part of the job. "Linkage" involves both development work and particularized benefits.

6. Despite the pressure to refrain from criticism, the

Minister of Plantation Industries, M.D.H. Jayawardene, spoke out against the government during the 1979 budget debate. He was demoted from minister to backbencher as a result of his speech. Since that time he has continued to speak critically of the government during debates.

7. This quotation and any other uncited quotation are taken from the interviews with the Sri Lankan MPs. If a quotation is taken from any other source, it will be noted in a footnote.

4
Political Demands

Demands in a political system are a means of linking the constituents with their government. They are also part of the interactive relationship between legislators and their constituents discussed in Chapter 1. In Sri Lanka the framework for making demands on legislators is highly institutionalized, and constituents find their legislators highly accessible. This chapter examines the nature of demands in Sri Lanka and the motivation that legislators have to respond to them. As mentioned earlier, constituents must have some means to punish or reward a legislator if their demands are to have any effect. Thus, it is hypothesised that the legislators believe that their electoral victory or defeat was largely a result of their action or inaction in response to the demands of their constituents. This however is not the case in Sri Lanka, as is shown in the second part of this chapter. The electoral success or defeat of Sri Lankan legislators is largely the result of factors that are beyond their control.

The first section of this chapter discusses the nature of political demands in Sri Lanka. Michael Mezey (1976) has developed a typology of political demands which divides them on the basis of who benefits from the demand and who makes it. Demands may be either generalized or particularized. Particularized demands are those whose primary consequences will affect an individual, a small group of people or a single organization. Generalized demands are those which may affect the country's population in general. Generalized demands may be divided into two sub-categories: (1) national demands which affect the nation as a whole or a significant region of it; and (2) local demands which are confined to the petitioner's district, municipality or electorate.

Demands may be made by individuals or groups. Groups may be local, based in a legislator's constituency, or they may be national with interests which are not limited to one constituency. Figure 4.1 depicts this typology of demands. The demand makers are capable

FIGURE 4.1
Types of demands made on legislators

Beneficiary of the Demand	Who Makes the Demand
Particularized	Individuals
General	Groups
National	National
Local	Constituency

of making any of the three types of demands. In addition, as Mezey (1976:104) has pointed out, these demands may be directed at many structures in the political system, "such as the bureaucracy, interest groups, political parties, local governmental institutions and local elites." The ability of other institutions to act on demands will affect the volume of demands that are directed toward the legislators.

In order to make demands on legislators, constituents must have access to the legislators. Most Sri Lankan MPs live in their constituencies and most meet frequently with their constituents and others from outside their electorates who seek an audience with them. All but two of the sample of legislators stated that they met regularly with their constituents. Most (64.1 percent) had days scheduled on which they would meet with their constituents and entertain their requests. These meetings were open to anyone who was willing to come and endure the lines waiting to see the member of

often begin their day at five or six a.m. and continue meeting with their constituents until ten or eleven p.m. Those who had no fixed day would usually begin their day meeting thirty to forty constituents waiting at the door to their house. The scene around most members' houses included small groups of people talking and waiting for the return of the MP and an opportunity to meet with him or her.

The amount of time that MPs spend in their electorates is an important indication of how accessible they are to their constituents. In Sri Lanka, the amount of time that the MPs spend in their electorates each month is a function of the formal authority they hold in parliament. Ministers and deputy ministers spend less time than backbenchers and opposition members (see Table 4.1). The ministers and deputy ministers found that they had to spend a great deal of time in their offices in Colombo tending to ministry business and, thus, had less time to spend in their electorates. It is interesting to note that the backbench rebels did not spend

TABLE 4.1
Average days spent by MPs in electorate per month

	Number	Average Days per Month
Ministers	18	11.2
Deputy Ministers[a]	17	12.8
Rebels	8	16.5
Backbenchers (excluding rebels)	36	21.6
Opposition	20	20.2

[a]The deputy minister category does not include the three district ministers who averaged twenty-two days a month in their electorates.

as much time in their electorates as did other backbenchers but tended to spend more time in their electorates than did the ministers and deputy ministers. This once again reflects their inability to accept the role of backbencher and their desire to have other national responsibilities.[1]

It should be noted that the MPs who did not spend a great deal of time in their electorates had other means of making themselves accessible to their constituents. A few ministers met with their constituents in Colombo although this practice was frowned upon by most ministers. Others would schedule days when they would be in their electorates. These days would be publicized and the MP involved would be prepared to meet for as many hours as was necessary to listen to the demands of all constituents who might come.

The meetings with the constituents were an integral part of the job of all MPs, including the ministers and deputy ministers. They were time consuming and demanding but accepted, even if grudgingly by the legislators.[2] The constituents appeared to expect these meetings as a part of the duty of a member. The wife of one MP stated, "My husband and I have been woken up in bed in the morning by a constituent walking into our bedroom seeking a favor." One MP complained, "One day while meeting with my constituents I had to answer a call of nature. While squatting there, I heard 'sir, sir, I think now is an excellent time to bring up a problem that has been bothering me.'" Several other MPs complained of people coming at all hours of the night to meet with them.

Organized groups also have easy access to the legislators. Both nationally and locally based organizations have little difficulty meeting with the minister or backbencher involved. Thus, the Sri Lankan legislators are highly accessible.[3]

Individuals coming to their legislators in Sri Lanka deal overwhelmingly with particularized demands (see Table 4.2). Only two members, who met with their constituents, did not cite particularized demands as the main reason for constituent visits. The overwhelming majority of the members cited jobs or job related demands[4] as the main reason their constituents came to see them. When the secondary reasons cited by the MPs are examined, the dominating influence of particularized benefits becomes clearer (see Table 4.3).

Most of the secondary reasons cited by the MPs dealt with such particularized requests as land needs, disputes over boundaries, water or other problems connected with cultivation. The local generalized demands included requests for roads, electricity and transportation facilities. However, many of the local generalized

TABLE 4.2
Main reasons why constituents come to MPs, as cited by MPs

	Number	Percent
Particularized Benefits	97	95.1
To Talk Politics or National Generalized Demands	2	2.0
Did Not Meet With Constituents	2	2.0
No Response	1	1.0
	102	100.1

Note: Totals in the percent column do not add up to one hundred percent due to rounding.

TABLE 4.3
Secondary reasons cited by MPs for constituents coming to them

	Number	Percent
Particularized	67	67.6
Generalized		
Local	19	19.2
National	1	1.0
No Second Reason Cited	35	35.4

Note: Totals exceed number in sample due to several members providing more than one response.

demands involved requests that would result in community improvement but were primarily intended to benefit the petitioner such as a road to one's house or electrification of an area surrounding one's house. Surprisingly, only one member cited national problems.

The members interviewed clearly believed that their constituents came to them for personal reasons. National and community oriented demands were not felt to be a serious part of the individual demands made on them. To further examine the types of individual demands that were made on the members, four meetings with MPs were observed and the reasons that constituents came were noted.[5] Of the petitioners whose reason for coming could be ascertained,[6] over 79 percent came looking for help to find a job, transfer or promotion (see Table 4.4). Only 2.8 percent came looking for something that could be described as community oriented and in each of these cases it involved a "community" development project that would directly benefit them. None came to the member with a concern based on national issues or legislation. Individual demands on the members were overwhelmingly personal in nature.

Although these findings are to be expected among the backbenchers, who as is shown in Chapter 6 do not deal with national issues, it is surprising that the ministers were not met with more national demands. The Sri Lankan electorate is highly literate and is generally considered to be knowledgeable about politics and national issues.

Although little evidence exists concerning the political interest and involvement of the Sri Lankan electorate, some general observations can be made.

TABLE 4.4
Constituent reasons for coming to meet with members in observed meetings

	Number	Percent
Jobs, Promotions, and Transfers	141	79.2
Government Benefits	8	4.5
Local Development	5	2.8
Other Reasons	24	13.5
Total	178	100.0

Electoral participation in the form of voter turnout in Sri Lanka is extremely high. Turnout in the 1977 parliamentary elections was 86.7 percent (Abeynaike, 1978: 219). Five years later in the first presidential election it was 81.1 percent (Wiswa Warnapala and Hewagama, 1983:63). In addition, evidence from another South Asian nation, India, indicates that the Indian electorate shows levels of political involvement, issue awareness, and political efficacy comparable to the United States and the countries of Western Europe (Eldersveld and Ahmed, 1978). The perceptions of the Sri Lankan MPs interviewed also supported this evidence. They felt that their election victory or loss was the result of national issues and not their own popularity. Many expressed a belief that their parliamentary speeches in newspapers and in published versions of the parliamentary speeches were of significance because large numbers of constituents read the speeches in newspapers and in published versions of the parliamentary debates. Sri Lankan newspapers in all three languages--Sinhala, Tamil and English--provide extensive coverage of the parliamentary debates, with portions of the debates reproduced in the newspapers. Thus, the Lankan electorate appears to have a wide interest in national politics and has access to information about national issues and their legislators.

The lack of concern with national issues may, in part, be the result of a lack of controversial issues at the national level which have significance to the people in the villages. The period of this study was devoid of highly charged issues that might have had a deep effect on village life. Several writers have noted that there was a great concern among the masses over the revival of Buddhism at the time of S.W.R.D. Bandaranaike's rise to power in the 1950s (Kearney, 1967:74-83; Phadnis, 1976:175-188; Wriggins, 1960:335-348). Constituency based groups and individuals pressured their MPs to act in support of their religion and culture. However, the forces that led to the Buddhist resurgence in the 1950s were not sustained and the concerns of the villagers returned to the economic reality of village life.[7]

Clearly, when individuals came to meet with the Sri Lankan MPs, they did it for personal reasons.[8] Individual petitioners do not stress community or national issues unless the issues benefit the petitioners themselves. Thus individual demands in Sri Lanka do not vary between the members with different positions of formal authority in parliament. They all receive, essentially, the same types of requests.

It has been argued that the emergence of interest groups is a part of modernization and the changes that accompany it (Almond and Powell, 1978:196-97). In Sri Lanka, interest groups are both unorganized and weak. This belief was strongly supported by all of the members interviewed. When asked about the pressure exerted on them, most spoke of the pressure of individuals to be unbearable and dismissed the influence of groups. Backbench members stated that national interest groups rarely came to them with requests. This reflects the limited power that the members have concerning national issues. The ministers appeared to receive more pressure from national interest groups than did the backbenchers and deputy ministers, but when asked about pressure, they usually complained about the individual pressure for particularized benefits and tended to dismiss group pressure as insignificant. Several ministers stated that they were rarely approached by national interest groups.

The potential pressure exerted by interest groups in Sri Lanka is limited by several factors. The first of these has been noted by Myron Weiner in India (Weiner, 1962:217). He argues that organized groups try to influence the administrative rather than the policy making process. Public policy in Sri Lanka is the result of a party platform and the party's ideology. Many groups know in advance that the government's ideology is not favorable to their demands and direct their demands to the administrators who may be more responsive and can circumvent the rules to assist their demand. This factor is limited by the general hostility of the political parties in Sri Lanka to what they call "sabotage by public officials" hostile to the governing party's platform (Kearney, 1973:83-84). Attempts have been made to transfer or suspend bureaucrats who may be sympathetic to the opposition party. There is a strong belief held by many politicians that bureaucrats work for either one of the major parties.

A second factor is that the major parties establish interest groups which they then are able to control (Weiner,1962:216). This reinforces the first factor since most interest groups will either be closely connected with the government or an opposition party and, thus, do not need access to the politicians. Interest groups in Sri Lanka are frequently extensions of political parties. This phenomena has been noted among Sri Lankan trade unions (Kearney, 1971; Wriggins, 1960) and religious groups (Phadnis, 1976; Smith, 1966:490-94). Kearney (1971:2) has noted that union leaders commonly believe that "the triumph of the party with which the union is associated" will lead to the union's political objectives. This tends to lead to an all or nothing view of the political process by the unions. Thus, if the wrong party is in power, the unions do not expect to receive government cooperation and benefits. In addition, they tend to lose members while trade unions affiliated with the government gain members. There is little bargaining and compromise, as is commonly found among interest groups in the United States. The organization either receives what it wants from its party when it is in power or its request is denied.

A third factor is that policy-making power is concentrated in a few important ministries and thus the number of people who may influence that policy is limited. The concentration of policy-making power is discussed in more depth in Chapter 6 (see Oberst, 1985).

A fourth factor is the nature of influence and power in Sri Lanka. Much pressure goes through family networks, friends or brokers (Jupp, 1978:194; Jiggins, 1979). Sri Lankans tend to view power in personal terms and when an individual, no matter how unimportant he may be, goes to a man or woman with power, he expects to meet personally with that man or woman. No representative of that person is acceptable or welcome. Access to power for them is a personal affair, and surrogates or letters will not be the same as meeting directly. Thus a lobbyist in Sri Lanka is effective only if he can establish a set of personal contacts. The highly partisan nature of politics in Sri Lanka makes it very difficult for an individual to maintain close personal contacts with powerful members of both parties.

A fifth factor is that interest groups tend to be ad hoc (Phadnis, 1976:273; Wriggins, 1960:252). Groups become active over an emotional issue and once their initial objective is achieved or the issue loses its emotional appeal, the groups become inactive. This is especially the case with village level organizations as is noted in Chapter 7.

All of the major parties have used interest groups to campaign for them or promote issues of concern to the party. Even when overt partisan ties are not maintained, some trade union leaders have been noted to actively support a political party.[9] The result is trade unions which are either supported by political parties and frequently headed by party leaders (Kearney, 1971:82) or by men allied to the parties.

The ministers interviewed reflected the interpersonal relationships that existed between themselves and the interest groups petitioning them. All stated that they did not feel pressured by the groups and that they maintained good relations with the organizations that came to see them. The establishment and maintenance of good relations with ministers seemed to mark the relationships between ministers and leaders of groups. It also reflected the highly personal nature of the relationships. The leadership of the groups was frequenty dominated by one dynamic individual. This has been found in the trade unions (Kearney, 1971: Chapter VII) and in the religious organizations of the Buddhist revival of the 1950s (Phadnis, 1976:273). The minister receiving nationally oriented group demands generally faces someone who has cultivated a personal relationship with him and who shares similar opinions and goals, and if they do have differences of opinion, the differences are not confronted by the two parties.

Facilitating this interpersonal relationship between the ministers and interest groups is the tendency for the creation of ministries that will cater to certain interests. For instance, the Ministry of Cultural Affairs was set up to deal with the demands of the All-Ceylon Buddhist Congress (Jupp, 1978:174). The political and bureaucratic appointments to the ministry are people who are favorably disposed toward the interest group or groups the ministry was created to serve.

The relationship between ministers and national interest groups is not one of compromise and bargaining but rather one of cooperation and accommodation. The effectiveness of these groups in affecting policy, although limited by poor organization, is increased by the close ties the groups have with political parties (in the case of trade unions) and the personal relationships created by the leaders of the groups with the members of parliament.

Local organizations function in a slightly different way. All members stated that they were approached by constituency based interest groups.[10] They generally agreed that the groups did not apply much pressure on them although many complained that the groups came seeking particularized benefits for individual members of the group. This was especially prevalent among the local party branches which often sought jobs, transfers and promotions for certain members of the branch. Among other types of local groups it was frequently stated that when representatives of the groups came to see the MPs, they would often interject the group request with personal requests. In some cases these personal requests went against the policy that the organization sought to have enacted. Another problem was stated by a member in this way:

> "People collect groups to do work. A rich man wants a road and he gets others who have no need for it to come as a group. So a large group comes (usually fifteen or so). Each one in the group has personal problems so they try to sneak it in while alone with the MP. They use the 'group' meeting as a vehicle to get an audience with the MP."

Thus, groups may only represent their leader and the so-called representatives of the group may come along only to present their own grievance and not that of the group.

Table 4.5 shows the groups and organizations cited by the members as frequently coming to them. It should

TABLE 4.5
Local organizations cited by members

	Number	Percent
Rural Development Societies	67	65.7
Party Branches	60	58.8
Religious	18	17.6
Cultivation Committees	14	13.7
Trade Unions	13	12.7
PTAs	12	11.8
Local Government	12	11.8
Cooperatives	10	9.8
No Response/Not Important	3	2.9

be noted that many of these groups are not what are often considered interest groups such as the local political party branches, yet the members perceive them as organizations representing different interests in their electorate and they have been included here. The most common groups cited were the rural development societies (RDS) and the local party branches. Almost two-thirds of the respondents stated that either one of these groups came to them frequently with requests. Most of the local party branches were set up by the member of parliament either while that member was attempting to gain office or after achieving it. The leadership of the organizations are therefore supporters of the MP and usually close to the member although the leaders generally are elected by the branch. In the two cases where the MP did not set up the local party branches or inherit them from a relative, the MPs had difficulties and disputes with the branches. In one case, the MP sought to hold elections as soon as possible to replace the leadership of the branches which were formed by that member's dead predecessor. In the other case, the LSSP member ignored the groups and was denied the opportunity to seek reelection in the next parliamentary elections by the LSSP.[11]

The rural development societies were originally created to foster development through community participation in development projects (Government of Sri Lanka, 1976:4-6). As is argued in Chapter 7, they are highly partisan and are generally led by a confidant of the local member of parliament.

The leadership of these two groups and most of the other groups listed in Table 4.5 are supporters of the members involved. As one member stated, "I can't call it pressure, I want to give them what they want but my resources are limited." The relationship is between a politician and his supporters. The interactions between the local groups and the MPs, like the national groups, are based on personal relationships between the leaders of the groups and the local MP. The pressure from these development oriented groups has grown in recent years since the institution of the decentralized budget, a system of transferring central revenues back to the local areas through the MP of that area.[12]

Both interest groups on the national level and the constituency based groups function in relatively similar ways. Their influence is based on personal relationships with the members involved. This results in the MP responding to the demands of "friends." The types of demands that the groups make on the MP are mediated by the influentials that lead the groups and often are not the product of mass pressure. The potential for mass involvement exists in each of the groups mentioned above, but in general that involvement is limited. In any case, the pressure is applied by individuals who appear as friends and not as representatives of groups.

The political demands placed on members of parliament in Sri Lanka are overwhelmingly personal in nature. Figure 4.2 depicts the typology of demands presented earlier with the volume of demands listed for each category. Particularized demands are frequently made by individuals, and moderately so among constituency based interest groups. National generalized demands are rarely ever made except by a few nationally based interest groups while local generalized demands are largely generated by constituency based interest groups.

As noted, Sri Lankan constituents make a large number of demands on their legislators. For these demands to have any effect on the legislators, the constituents must have some way to punish those legislators who do not respond to their demands and reward those who do. This can be done by denying the MP re-election. It was clearly established in the interviews that Sri Lankan members of parliament do not rely heavily on outside campaign funds. Thus, voters and interest groups are not in a position to deny their legislators campaign funds. However, the defeat of sitting MPs is quite common in Sri Lanka. In the elections to the Seventh and Eighth Parliaments, well over 50 percent of the incumbents lost in their re-election bid.

When the members in the sample were asked why they had won or lost their last election, over two-thirds (67.9 percent) of the 78 responding stated that it was because of the policies or record of one of the parties contesting the election. Under thirty (29.5) percent stated that it was due to factors in their constituencies. When asked what was the most important factor in determining the vote of their constituents, 55.2 percent of the ninety-six responding stated that their political party was the most important factor while only

FIGURE 4.2
Frequency of demands made on legislators

		Individuals	Who Makes Them	Groups
Nature Of The Consequences Of The Demand			Constituency	National
Particularized		High	Moderate	Low
General	National	Low	Low	Moderate
	Local	Low	High	Low

32.3 percent stated that it was their policies or personality.[13] Over 12 percent either stated that it was caste or that the factors were all equal.

Thus, it would appear that the personal style of the MPs or their actions in their electorates do not play a large part in how their electorates vote.[14] Rather, the record of their party or the party in office is believed to be the deciding factor in the elections. Since most of the MPs have little input into the policy making process (see Chapter 6), it would appear that the MPs do not have much control over whether they are re-elected or not. It would also indicate that they are spending most of their time and effort on a job, constituency service and development work, without that time and effort affecting their chances of re-election.

An explanation of this phenomenon may lie in one of several possibilities. The first is that the members are not able to supply enough jobs to their constituents and thus are being defeated because they fail to meet their demands. (The next chapter deals with job requests in more detail.) This would appear to be unlikely. The number of jobs supplied by the members was relatively high. A large number of MPs claimed to have supplied between five and seven thousand jobs during their term of office.[15] This number may appear to be relatively large; however, the total undoubtedly includes temporary employment and jobs with low status such as manual labor. In addition, when the size of the unemployed and underemployed population in each electorate is considered (probably about ten to fifteen thousand), this number does not appear that large.

Yet, most MPs stated that their government's or the other party's record in office was the main factor influencing their election. In doing this they cited corruption, the cost of living, and the scarcity of consumer products as factors, but most did not mention the job situation. Thus, although the constituents might have reason to be disappointed with the performance of their MPs in supplying them with jobs, a few MPs felt that the lack of jobs was an important factor in the election results.

A second explanation for this phenomenon arises from the culture and traditions of Sri Lankan society. It would appear that both the Sri Lankan people and their leaders relate to leadership in a very personal way. The MP is viewed as a father and projects the image of a patron or a friend in times of need.[16] It is this response to duty that motivates most MPs. The constituents expect the MPs to deal with their personal problems while the MPs believe, in most cases, that this is their responsibility. This relationship is described in more depth in the following section. It is argued that traditional attitudes toward authority in Sri Lanka have influenced the nature of present day legislator-constituent relationships. (For a similar argument see Levy, 1974.) This is not to say that Sri Lankans view authority the same way that their ancestors did but rather to argue that these traditional attitudes have been superimposed on a modern political system. It might be said that it is similar to the sense of frontier individualism that is expressed in the culture of the United States today and has some influence on the political behavior of Americans. These traditional attitudes create a climate where legislators are expected to respond to the demands of their constituents, even if that response is not rewarded with re-election. The reward is a psychic one--the knowledge that the members have fulfilled their duties and responsibilities in a just way.[17]

It is argued in this section that Sri Lankan MPs view their job as a duty[18] and that their constituents have similar expectations about their leaders and that these structure the behavior and attitudes of the legislators. Thus, what has happened, has been the transference of the roles from traditional sources of power and authority to the members of parliament.

At the height of the British Empire, Ceylon, as it was then called, was considered to be the "senior" crown colony of the empire and thus was entrusted with certain rights that other colonies were denied (Wight, 1946: 74).[19] In 1910 it became the first colony in which there were elected non-European representatives on the legislative council (Wight, 1946:78), and in 1931 it was the first Asian country to receive universal adult suffrage. This was only three years after Great Britain granted universal adult suffrage to its citizens (Namasivayam, 1950:55). The early establishment of the potential for popular participation in the government firmly established the role of the masses in dealing with their government. Today, Lankans are attached to their heritage of representative democracy and firmly believe in the concept of popular control over their representatives.

The establishment of the rudiments of parliamentary democracy in Sri Lanka was superimposed over traditional beliefs and attitudes toward authority and political leadership. The creation of a "modern" political state did not necessarily change the way in which the people responded to their leaders. An important element in the masses' relationship with their leaders is a general subservience to any authority (Wood, 1961:22). This attitude is so ingrained in the people that it has been cited as a reason for political stability in post-colonial Sri Lanka (Wood, 1961:22) and as a reason why "true democracy will never exist in Sri Lanka."[20] Wood attributes the relative ease the British had in ruling Ceylon to this deference to authority by the peasants and the buying off of the elite with prestigious appointments.[21] This was a continuation of the state of affairs that had existed prior to the arrival of the Europeans where "It was the duty of the subjects...to be obedient...and subordinate.... The very concept of king, raja, implies authority; loyalty and subordination are the complimentary attributes of the King-subject relation [sic]" (Gunasekera, 1978:130). The people were treated as children in need of a protector (Gunasekera, 1978:133). They would come to him to raise questions of injustice in their village dealings with his representatives (Gunasekera, 1978; Knox, 1956-57:84). The king's subjects were to be docile acceptors of the will of the ruling class. In a highly stratified society where occupations are ascriptive, it is to be expected that people will be very accepting of those who are a part of the ruling class. The ruling class is not something one aspires to but rather is born into.

Authority and power were derived from the leaders in such a way that the people have a very poorly developed notion of the delegation of authority (De Silva, 1953:172). This is not to say that the people would accept everything ordered by the ruling elite and sit silently as a despotic king dictated their lives. The king was expected to do certain things. "It was...the tradition among the Sinhala people to consider whether a King was dharmista..., righteous, or not.... The King was expected by the subjects to rule with a sense of fairness" (Gunasekera, 1978:133; also see Levy, 1973:13). The historical accounts of the Kandyan kingdom are full of rebellion, although frequently the avenue to rebellion was through the allegiance to other leaders who received the same deference and respect (Knox, 1956:57-92 and Gunasekera, 1978:137-39). The peasants required a very strong justification before they would go against the tradition of deference and subordination, and revolt against their leaders.

Another factor that affected the continuation of traditional responses to leadership was the nature of the administrative apparatus that existed just prior to the arrival of the British, and the adaptations that the British made to this apparatus after taking control of Sri Lanka. Prior to the colonial era, the King's authority was diffused among the ruling elite who assisted him in his rule. An elaborate system of administration existed in the Kandyan Kingdom shortly before it was conquered by the British (Knox, 1956-57:Chapter V). The representatives of the king were the embodiment of the authority and power of the king over his subjects (Gunasekera, 1978:135). These people not only administrated the king's raj but acted as a judicial authority as well (De Silva, 1953:295). There was no distinction between the one who made the rules, administrated them, and arbitrated the disputes arising from their use. The king's administrators were made up of a dominant caste and oversaw the local administration in the rural areas (Gunasekera 1978:135). In these areas, high caste, large landlords dominated the power structure. A peasant with a grievance risked the alienation of the rural elite if he appealed to a higher authority (De Silva 1953:299).

The arrival of the British brought a new system. The British worked to reduce the power and influence of the local leaders (De Silva, 1953:197,263). At the same time they tried to transfer the royal authority from the king of Kandy to the British monarch. European control superimposed new institutions on the traditional system of administration and government (De Silva, 1953:299). The British sought to use the village headman as the link between the government and the people[22] (Samaraweera, 1973:43). This resulted in a large dependence by the British on the headman for liaison with the people (Wickremeratne, 1973:166). Thus, the Queen of England replaced the Kandyan royal family as monarch, and her administrators were now located in the larger urban centers of the island. The British administrators were largely ignorant of the customs, languages and culture of the Sri Lankan people (Wickremeratne, 1973:166) and the citizenry no longer had the higher authorities to go to for redress of their grievances. The new system was alien to them and the result was a sense of impotency and confusion. The new rulers were distant and exercised their power in a way that was alien to the peasant.

Thus, the traditional power structure was marked by a certain amount of deference to authority in which the masses accepted the rule of the king as long as their basic needs were taken care of. The rule of the king was exercised by influentials spread out through the rural communities. The political system imposed by the British failed to change the nature of relationships between the masses and political elites (Wood, 1961:99). At the time of independence, the citizenry still expected their leaders to take care of their basic needs in a paternalistic way and continued to respond to authority and leadership in ways dictated by earlier patterns of culture and tradition.

Indications of the continuing effects of the culture and traditions of the Sri Lankan people can still be seen in the present day constituent-legislator relationships. The members of parliament continue to act as the loyal representative of governmental authority.

Their actions are in coordination with the wishes of the leaders. Only those members who are loyal to the executive power can be expected to help a petitioner. The president, under the constitution of 1978 and the prime minister under the earlier constitutions frequently have drawn from the traditional sources of authority. In recent years they have made a strong effort to display their ties with Buddhism. Historically, Buddhism was closely associated with the political power of the country (Siriwardene, 1966:537; Kodikara, 1970:100-106). Today, it is very common for bhikkhus (Buddhist priests) to appear on the speaker's platforms at election rallies and political events. Politicians make a strong effort to display their devotion to the Buddha. Newly appointed ministers travel to the Temple of the Tooth in Kandy where the most sacred relic of Sri Lankan Buddhism is kept--a tooth of the Buddha--to pay homage before it. It is an act showing the symbolic tie between the government and the Buddhist religion. The symbolism of the act was vividly shown in 1978 when a recently appointed Tamil minister, Sauvmiamoorthy Thondaman, a Hindu not a Buddhist, made his pilgrimage to the relic and paid homage at the Buddhist shrine. Under the presidential system, the use of symbolism has been even more apparent. The president wields nearly as much executive power as the Kandyan kings of an earlier era, and easily commands the authority and respect of the populace. It is no surprise that the first president of the new Democratic Socialist Republic of Sri Lanka refers to his government as the <u>dharmista</u> (righteous) government. He takes an active part in important religious ceremonies and tries to promote the image of a man above the internecine squabbles of politics.

Another indication of the continuing effects of the traditional attitudes toward power can be seen in the relationship between the constituents and their members of parliament. Two dissenters to a government report in the 1930s reveal their perception of the average Sri Lankan's attitude toward authority and government. They stated that "government means little or nothing [to the villagers]. They have always been accustomed by tradition and temperament to seek and obey the orders of personal representatives of a personal sovereign and receive the personal care and protection of accessible and paternal rulers" (Nugawela and Wedderburn, 1935). Apparently there was a need among the people for a fatherly figure who would oversee their well being as was done in the era of the Kandyan kings. One MP echoed a similar and more modern statement of this. "They [the constituents] want someone to rule them in the family. Voters want the same. They want to go to someone for help. They want someone to go to."

Under the British colonial administration, villagers had the choice of two people to go to for assistance. These were their local headman, and the district government agent or his assistants. Over the last thirty years, the responsibilities and role of the headman and government agent have been taken over by the MP.

The headmen functioned in the role of government representatives. They prepared lists of the people who needed relief, conducted prosecutions in court, settled minor grievances and disputes between families, distributed rice to the poor, oversaw government licenses, and arranged for other necessities of people in need (Government of Sri Lanka [Ceylon], 1935). At the time of independence, the headmen served the functions of ombudsman and surrogate parent to a people who no longer had their king or his representatives to oversee them, but rather a distant and alien colonial administration. The headmen served both the administrative and judicial functions of a governmental authority.

Beginning in the 1930s, the administrative setup was slowly transformed. It was believed that the headmen exerted their power in an arbitrary and corrupt way. The first action was to change the name of the chief headman to divisional revenue officer. In addition, vacancies in the post were replaced by open competition after 1938 (Kearney, 1966:525). In the 1960s the village headmen were replaced by grama sevakas who were appointed after competitive exam and were transferable from one place to another (Kearney, 1966:525). With these changes, the headmen lost much of their power. They were no longer the hereditary leaders of the area, who commanded authority on the basis of their traditional position. Because they had been an economic power in their villages, they had been able to back up their authority with actions that would affect the lives of the people. The changes in the system removed many of the traditional sources of authority of the headmen and stripped them of much of their power. The new system emerged gradually because of the replacement of the traditional leaders by attrition only. After the new system was firmly established the people lost one of their potential sources of help in times of need and in facing bureaucratic red tape.[23]

Another important factor in the paternalistic government of the colonial era was the government agent. The government agent was the highest ranking government official in the administrative districts.[24] At first he was a revenue agent but gradually became a "jack of all trades" (Leitan, 1976:16-17). As the overseer of all government operations in his area of authority, he became the final arbiter of disputes and problems. On the death of one government agent in the nineteenth century, a Colombo newspaper stated, "Mr. Dyke was in every sense a Rajah in Jaffna, and the people invariably treated him as such. They knew they were safe in his hands..." (Ceylon Observer, October 14, 1867). The government agent of the colonial era served many of the functions of a paternalistic lord. When the villagers could not get satisfaction in their disputes, they would go to him. The office of the government agent was frequently surrounded by people of the district waiting to petition him. At other times the government agent would hold "division days." This was a day on which the government agent or assistant government agent would hold court in an area, seeing the local populace, listening to their needs and questioning the government officials involved (Kahawita, 1979:10).

Immediately prior to independence, the administrative structure was changed with the establishment of cabinet ministries. Each ministry had responsibility over departments throughout the island. Vertical systems of administration were created where the department heads in the districts owed allegience and responsibility to the ministry in Colombo and not the GA of the district (Fernando, 1973:21). This trend was aggravated by the power of the ministries in Colombo and the association of the "kachcheri" system of administration[25] with colonialism. Following the SLFP victory in 1956, a shift was made away from the kachcheri and its agents to the departments in the districts and their main offices in Colombo (Fernando, 1973:23). The period after the Donoughmore Constitution of 1931 and into the independent era was marked by a general decline in the power and influence of the government agent (Fernando, 1973:18). His ability to shape the lives of the individual villagers had sharply declined, although he still wielded considerable power in the district.

The decline of the colonial system of administration and the government agent was accompanied by a new current of thought; the ideal of equality of treatment that emerged after the SLFP victory in 1956. Its roots were in the granting of independence and the ideology of democracy. The high levels of literacy allowed it to catch on quickly and the SLFP's appeal to the rural masses in 1956 revealed to the masses that they had the ability to change the leadership in Colombo. The people came to believe that the government existed to serve

them and to foster their well being. They had a right
to request and expect help from their government representatives, and as is shown in Chapter 5, they have done
this.

The creation of a parliamentary system based on
universal suffrage under the Donoughmore Constitution of
1931 gave the populace their first real opportunity to
be represented by legislators. The result "was a tendency among constituents of members of the state council
to turn to them for advice and assistance, instead of
going to their headmen" (Collins, 1966:480). The state
council legislators provided an alternative power source
to whom the constituents could go to for help.

The power of the state legislative council members
was limited by the British. Upon the advent of independence, members of the legislature of the new independent state were given much more power. They had a
fair amount of discretion on how to direct development
projects in their electorates and had some patronage
jobs available. This was at a time when the power of
the headmen and government agents was declining. The
election of 1956 established a competitive party system
and in the context of competition, the parties now had
to cater to the voters. The representatives in the
legislature were eager to respond to constituent
requests in order to protect their position in parliament. In 1959, the electoral constituencies were redistricted and the number of constituencies were increased
from 89 to 145. The smaller constituencies meant that
the lawmakers could have much closer contact with their
electorates.

Thus, power was shifting from the colonial institutions of authority, especially the government agent[26]
to the members of parliament, while the members were
representing smaller constituencies and thus were closer
to the people they represented. At the same time a competitive party system was emerging along with an ideology of egalitarianism that provided an environment where
the legislators were responsive to the demands of the
people and the people felt that they had a right to
expect action from their representatives.

Thus, the Sri Lankan member of parliament assumed
the role once played by the traditional leadership of
Sri Lanka. They became the link between the people and
the government bureaucracy. Their responsibility is a
paternalistic one. The people expected it of them and
they accepted that role. It is generally believed that
legislators act to win votes and insure their position
in parliament in the next election. However, this does
not explain all of their behavior. In Sri Lanka they
are motivated by other forces--the demands of culture
and tradition.

The next three chapters examine the work of the
legislators in each of the three components of their job

as members of parliament. The following chapter considers the legislator's job as a provider of services to their constituency.

NOTES

1. A.J. Wilson has commented in personal correspondence that this may also reflect the "rebels" resignation to their not being renominated by their party in the next election.
2. The attitudes of the legislators toward meeting with their constituents will be discussed in the next chapter.
3. MPs frequently receive money in return for the favors they do for their constituents. The exchange of money often affects the outcome of the constituent's request but does not appear to affect access to the MPs. Corruption is discussed in Chapter 5.
4. Job related requests include requests for transfers and promotions. Unless otherwise noted, reference to job seekers includes those seeking transfers and promotions.
5. The four members included two cabinet ministers and two government backbenchers.
6. The meetings tend to be unruly with the petitioners crowding around the member's table with several making their requests at the same time while the MP or his or her staff are trying to process an earlier petitioner's request. As a result, it was not possible to ascertain the demands made by some petitioners.
7. It can be argued that among the Sri Lanka Tamils of the north and east there was a galvanizing issue during the period of the study. This issue was their perception of Sinhalese discrimination against them. However, there was no evidence that the Sri Lanka Tamils came to their representatives with generalized demands.
8. Jha (1977:133) notes that in the Indian state of Bihar constituent pressure is largely for personal reasons with little pressure for laws.
9. The leaders of two of the largest "independent" trade unions have been appointed to parliament as MPs by the governing party. One later won election as the candidate of the political wing of his union and then accepted a cabinet portfolio in the Eighth Parliament.
10. Constituency based groups for the purposes of this analysis include the local branches of trade unions while national groups include the central leadership of the unions.
11. The member involved claimed that he did not seek re-election for other reasons.
12. The budget is discussed in more depth in Chapter 7.
13. Caste did not appear to play a major role in electoral choice. In most electorates, the major parties nominated candidates of the same caste. Most MPs estimated that their electorates were populated by over 70 percent of their caste.
14. Goodman (1975) has found that constituency service work did not help South Vietnamese legislators in their re-election attempts.
15. This is an area where widespread corruption has occurred.

Corruption is discussed in Chapter 5.

16. Traditionally this relationship could be described as a patron-client relationship (see Scott, 1972). However, the changes brought by modernization and the establishment of a parliamentary democracy have severely weakened the relationship to the point where the clients do not feel bound to the patron.

17. The United National Party government elected in 1977 has described their government as "<u>dharmista</u>" or just.

18. Goodman (1967:87) argues that American legislators in the nineteenth century had a similar sense of duty about their responsibilities in Congress.

19. An example of how ethno-centric the British were toward their empire can be seen in Wight's (1946:74) statement that Ceylon was "the only non-European colony with a pre-existing civilization, as contrasted with primitive societies."

20. An influential former Sri Lankan government minister stated in private correspondence with the author that the people of Sri Lanka will never stand up and fight for their rights and thus will have little control over their destiny.

21. The revolt of 1848 was the only serious threat to British control of the country.

22. There were several levels of authority for headmen ranging from the village level to the level of the <u>rata</u> (district). They existed prior to the arrival of the European powers and were maintained by the British with some adaptation. Their functions included administrative, judicial and legislative responsibilities.

23. The headmen often used their power in a very arbitrary manner and thus, many villagers saw them as potential oppressors as well as potential sources of help.

24. At first there was one GA for each province.

25. The kachcheri system is that arrangement of administration with the government agent in charge of a district and the government offices in that district under his oversight. It has been noted that the system did not evolve into a development oriented institution (Wiswa Warnapala, 1974:356-58) and thus has received a great deal of criticism over its weaknesses in this area. Changes begun in 1977 have increased the kachcheri's development orientation. This is discussed in Chapter 7.

26. Farmer (1962:71-72) argues that the MP has assumed the role of the government agent, assistant government agent and divisional revenue officer. Jupp (1978:229) argues that the MP took over the government agent's position, thus, making the MP a local chieftan.

5
Constituency Service

Constituency service was cited as the most time consuming aspect of a Sri Lankan legislator's job. This chapter examines the nature of the relationship between the members and their constituents as it pertains to the granting of particularized benefits. The first section looks at the growth of constituent demands for particularized benefits and the causes of it. This is followed by an analysis of the legislators' attitudes and behavior concerning the granting of particularized benefits. In Chapter 1 it was argued that the formal authority of a legislator affects the magnitude of the demands placed on the legislator. In addition, the nature and magnitude of demands made of all legislators are a function of external factors in the society.

Each of the respondents was asked to estimate the number of constituents coming to see them. Their responses indicated that the number of constituents coming to meet with their MPs in Sri Lanka for particularized benefits is extremely high. The average number of constituents seen per week for those members interviewed from the Eighth Parliament was just under 561 while in the Seventh Parliament it was over 448. In the Eighth Parliament this represents an average of about 29,214 constituents coming each year to meet with their member of parliament. At the time of the 1977 general elections, the average constituency had 37,164 voters. Thus, the average member of parliament meets with close to the total number of voters in his or her electorate in one year. Of course, many of those coming to see the MP come several times or are constituents from other electorates. Nevertheless, several MPs from the Seventh Parliament estimated that they had met personally with over 99 percent of their constituents at some time during their term of office.

The general impression of the MPs who had served in earlier parliaments was that the number of people coming to meet with them had increased sharply since they first entered parliament. Evidence of this is found in the responses by the MPs to the question asking them to estimate how many people came in an average week. The number of MPs giving responses for parliaments before the Seventh and Eighth Parliaments is somewhat limited, but even the scanty figures available give some impression of the increase. Table 5.1 reports the average number of constituents seen by each MP for several time periods. It indicates a very sharp increase in the number of people coming to meet with the members.

This increase in the number of constituents coming to meet with their members is the result of several factors converging in the 1960s and acting to increase the number of demands made on the members. As is mentioned in the last chapter, the Sri Lankan members of parliament have assumed many of the roles and responsibilities of local traditional leaders in the rural areas of the country. Several other phenomena which have led to a sharp increase in the number of demands placed on the legislators have accompanied the decline in the powers of the local headmen, government agents, and traditional leaders in the rural areas. The first of these trends has been the growth of government. As the size and scope of government grew, so did the number of benefits that it had at its disposal. The election of 1956 led to a more active role by the government in the economy of the country.

From 1958 to 1975 the number of state business enterprises nearly quadrupled in number, rising from 28 to 107 (Subasinghe, 1977:52). The value of capital invested in the enterprises increased from 72 million rupees to over 1,300 million rupees between 1956 and 1975.[1] This increase in government corporations and expanded role of the government led to an increased number of government jobs. At the same time, government welfare schemes were expanding. Expenditures on transfer payments increased from 621 million rupees in 1960 to almost 2,800 million rupees in 1975. As a percentage of total government expenditure, this was an increase from about 38 percent in 1960 to 51 percent in 1975 (Jayamaha, 1976:79).[2] Most of these increases have been in the area of education, health and food subsidies. In the area of education alone, the number of school teachers increased from just over thirty-five thousand in 1949 (Government of Sri Lanka [Ceylon], 1951:xxxi) to more than one hundred ten thousand in 1976 (Government of Sri Lanka, 1977:423). This growth in government not only increased the number of government jobs, but also meant an increased number of difficulties with bureaucratic redtape. Thus the populace had a greater need for help dealing with these problems.

The second factor was the growth of a competitive party system. The MPs felt that they must cater to the needs of the people in order to remain in office. Thus, after 1956 and the emergence of the SLFP as a

TABLE 5.1
Average number of constituents meeting with MPs per week

	Parliaments			
	Second & Third	Fifth & Sixth	Seventh	Eighth
Average	186.2	274.7	448.4	561.8
Number of Respondents	4	10	52	44

competitive force in Sri Lankan politics, both parties felt an electoral need to cater to the demands of the people. Patronage became an important part of Sri Lankan politics. The way in which patronage has intruded into the political arena is brought out later in this chapter and in Chapter 7.

The third factor was a general increase in the needs of the people. This was especially the case regarding employment. The educational system had grown and had been quite successful in educating large numbers of young people while at the same time lifting their aspirations for white collar jobs. School enrollment rose from under one million in 1946 (International Labour Organization, 1971:9) to over two and one-half million in 1976 (Government of Sri Lanka, 1979:429). After 1946, the introduction of DDT in the fight against malaria resulted in a very sudden and sharp decrease in the death rate on the island (Abeysundere, 1976:51-52; International Labour Office, 1971:9). This drop in the death rate resulted in a rapid surge in population growth as the infant death rate declined and life expectancy increased. The drop in the infant death rate resulted in a baby boom which, coupled with the growth of the educational system, resulted in a sudden increase of educated young people entering the labor market beginning in the late 1960s. Between 1946 and 1971, the labor force increased by over 72 percent (Government of Sri Lanka [Ceylon], 1951:xlii; Government of Sri Lanka, 1974:128). Forty percent of this increase occurred between 1963 and 1971 when the labor force grew by just over one million workers.

The economy was unable to increase the number of new jobs to match the number of youths joining the job market and very strong competition developed for the few jobs available. The consequences of this were soon felt by the MPs who were inundated by the seekers of particularized benefits. This increase in constituent demands has been, in large part, the result of this convergence of the shift of power from the colonial centers of authority in the society to the MPs and the growth of government coupled with a large surge in the number of youths entering the job market.

It was expected that the ability of a member of parliament to respond to particularized demands would affect the number of demands that were made on him or her (Mezey, 1978:150-151). Thus, the more able members are to satisfy demands, the more likely people will come to them. In Sri Lanka, law-making power resides in the hands of the cabinet ministers (see Chapter 6). In addition, all government jobs originate in some ministry. The ministers in charge of a ministry are more likely to have jobs at their disposal than backbenchers or opposition members. Table 5.2 reports that considerably more people went to the ministers than to other members of parliament. In the Eighth Parliament, the ministers averaged almost 1,200 constituent visits a week or over twice as many as the backbenchers' averaged. In the Seventh Parliament the differential between ministers and backbenchers was less, but was still substantial. The difference between backbenchers and deputy ministers was small in the Eighth Parliament. However in the Seventh Parliament, the backbenchers averaged a few more people coming to see them each week. This may be a reflection of the equality of power between the deputy ministers and backbenchers. The deputy ministers may have status but they have few patronage jobs. Opposition members saw considerably fewer people than did any of the government members. Once again this may reflect the inability of the opposition members to provide their constituents with patronage.

Those ministers who presented a large number of bills to parliament or presided over ministries which had large numbers of patronage jobs at their disposal tended to have more people coming to see them[3] (see Tables 5.3 and 5.4). In the Seventh Parliament, those ministers who presided over ministries with few patronage jobs averaged about the same number of people coming to see them as did the deputy ministers or backbenchers. In the Eighth Parliament, both categories of ministers averaged considerable more meetings with constituents than did the backbenchers and deputy ministers.

Those members with the greatest amount of patronage and policy-making power in the government claimed the highest number of constituents coming to see them with requests. Even among the ministers there appeared to be a hierarchy of more and less powerful members with the ministers of the more important ministries, both in policy making and in the number of patronage jobs available to them, receiving more constituents.

Although the evidence is based on limited data, the growth of the number of people coming to visit the MPs can be seen in each of the three government member categories (Table 5.2). What is significant is the failure

TABLE 5.2
Average number of constituents seen per week by MPs

	Parliaments					
	Prior to Seventh		Seventh		Eighth	
	Average	no.	Average	no.	Average	no.
Ministers	500.0	1	586.7	9	1192.9	7
Deputy Ministers	105.0	1	442.7	9	655.0	10
Backbenchers	233.0	5	463.8	26	539.6	13
Opposition	253.1	7	270.0	8	216.5	13
Total	253.0	14	448.4	52	561.8	43

TABLE 5.3
Policy influence of ministers and number of constituents coming

	Seventh Parliament		Eighth Parliament	
	Number	Average	Number	Average
High	5	652	2	1600
Low	4	512.5	5	1030

TABLE 5.4
Patronage power of ministry and number of constituents coming

	Seventh Parliament		Eighth Parliament	
	Number	Average	Number	Average
Large Number of Patronage Jobs	4	767.5	2	1600
Few Jobs	5	442	5	1030

Note: The high patronage ministries are Food and Cooperatives, Power, Highways, Local Government, Industries, and Buildings.

of the number of people coming to the opposition members to increase. This again is a reflection of the linkage between power and demands. The ability of the opposition members to assist their constituents is determined by the help they get from the government party, and thus they are not able to respond to an increased number of demands. The populace realizes this and does not come to them. Many members who had left their parties for another party while still in parliament stated that as soon as they left the government party, the number of people coming to see them had declined while those who joined the government party stated that the number increased. One stated that "the people think that we can't help them and so they do not come to us."

Another indication of the relationship between power and the number of constituents coming to meet with the MPs can be seen when the numbers coming to the "rebels" are analyzed. The seven backbench rebels in the Seventh Parliament averaged about 435 people per week. This is slightly less than the average for the backbenchers. Their attitudes may have resembled the ministers but their patronage power was no greater than that of the backbenchers, and their constituents realizing this did not come to them in as large numbers as the constituents of the ministers.

An analysis of the amount of mail the members estimate that they receive also tends to support the thesis that the level of demands is a result of the power of the member (see Table 5.5). The analysis was hampered by the fact that many ministers leave the handling and receipt of mail to their staff and thus do not know how much comes to them each week. Those ministers who responded to the question may have been those who receive the smallest amount of mail, and thus handle what comes themselves. This may indicate why Table 5.5 reports that in the Eighth Parliament deputy ministers received more mail than the ministers. In any case, the ministers and deputy ministers in both parliaments received far more mail than the backbenchers.

When compared to other countries, these figures are quite large.[4] This is surprising considering the great value that the Sri Lankans appear to place on personal contact with their MPs. Many members dismissed the number of letters sent to them as insignificant because (1) most constituents desire to appear personally before the MP and (2) the small size of the constituencies and excellent transportation facilities in the rural areas make travel to the MP's house or office relatively easy. (3) In addition, many of the letters were a follow-up to a personal visit to the MP, and either thanked him for his assistance or reiterated the petitioner's need for help.

It was noted in Chapter 4 that most of the individual requests made of Sri Lankan MPs were particularized in nature. The highly personalized relationships between the members of parliament and their constituents, described earlier in Chapter 4, has led to requests which are highly personal. One member, who spent almost thirty years in parliament, stated "as a long time member you become a father figure." Requests

TABLE 5.5
Formal authority and amount of mail received per week

	Parliament			
	Seventh		Eighth	
	Number	Average	Number	Average
Ministers	2	337.5	3	283.3
Deputy Ministers	7	282.1	7	341.4
Backbenchers	20	225.8	11	228.5
Opposition	6	121.7	7	150.4

ranged from women coming to the MP to ask his help because their husbands are sleeping with other women to members of the same family seeking the MP's help in resolving a family feud. At the same time the requests took a more conventional nature, at least more conventional in the eyes of westerners: constituents denied food ration books came seeking help in obtaining them; parents seeking help in getting their child admitted to a prestigious school; farmers seeking permits to cultivate plots of jungle; or those seeking the MP's intercession in criminal cases.

Despite the apparent trivial nature of most of the requests, the members took them quite seriously. The ministers, who were endowed with ample staff, would set up an office with three or four clerks working to assist the members as they met with their constituents. The constituents would line up for hours outside the door of the office. A police officer often would be present to keep the crowd under control. As the constituents entered the office, usually in groups of ten to twenty petitioners, they would wait in line to speak with the minister. In one of the two meetings with ministers that were observed, the petitioners spent an average of less than one and one-half minutes with the minister. (In the other observed meeting with a minister, the average was just under three minutes.) The constituents would then wait as a typist prepared a letter for them or a clerk attempted to telephone a bureaucrat or employer concerning their request. In some cases the petitioners name would be taken down and the minister would follow the request up later.

The backbenchers observed during their meetings did not have the benefit of several staff members but generally followed a similar pattern except they did not have the authority to claim the telephone lines so that they could make connections on their telephone calls.[5] Thus many problems had to wait until the MP had time to take the matter up later. The large numbers of petitioners made it very difficult for members to establish personal relationships with their constituents when they came to see them. The endless faces resulted in every attempt by the members to dispose of the requests as quickly as possible. In some cases, the tension of the day would result in the members losing their temper, or a dissatisfied petitioner breaking down in tears. In several cases the petitioners were told to leave and stop bothering the member. In one instance, a minister began berating a woman who had come for the thirteenth time looking for a job for her son who the minister felt was totally unqualified for the position.

> Your request is stupid. You come to the minister with stupid requests and bother him so that he cannot get his work done. Do you see this foreigner over here? He is writing a book. Do you know what he is going to write? He is going to say that you came to the Honourable Minister with stupid requests, and for all eternity people will know that you came to the minister with stupid requests and interfered with his important work.

The woman lowered her eyes in deference to his authority and with a terrified look on her face, quickly made her way to the door.

Many of the backbenchers would follow up the requests made of them. Several stated that when they were in Colombo for meetings of parliament, most of their time would be spent going from one office to another resolving requests. On two occasions, during the observed meetings between the ministers and their constituents, backbenchers came to the minister with a request.

The main response that the members were called upon to make was to find jobs for the unemployed and underemployed. This was an impossible task; there were far more job seekers than there were job openings. Many of the petitioners returned several times to ask if the member of parliament had had any luck in finding them a job or to report that they were still waiting for a job interview. Several members estimated that about 25 percent of the people who came to them were repeaters. A youth in a hill country city stated that during the first eighteen months of his MP's term, he had gone nine times to the member seeking employment. Each time he was told that there was nothing available for people with his qualifications.

The large number of people involved made it hard for the members to take a personal interest in how they responded. Each face looked the same in the long lines of endless faces that came before the member. In order to make a better impression with the member, many constituents would resort to intermediaries. Some members refused to allow intermediaries into the meetings, however most had no policies governing their use. In the case of one minister, the petitioners were screened at the door and in all but three cases, the person seeking the request was the only one allowed to enter. In the case of one of the backbenchers, the meeting hall had two to three brokers who used their personal influence with the member to bring people to her.

Among the three members who did allow people to accompany the petitioners, 28.6 percent of the petitioners came with someone else. This included over 19 percent of the males and 50 percent of the females. This reflects the role of women in the society and the belief that they need someone to help them and accompany them when they go to the MP to seek a job. One-third of the women came with their mother or father. In two cases, their father or brother came without them to press their case for a job. In the case of the female member observed meeting with her constituents, 90 percent of the women coming to her came with someone else.[6] Perhaps the constituents felt that because she was a woman, they must respond to her in more traditional ways and accompany their daughters when they went to meet with the MP. Among the males coming with someone else, most came with a friend or brother who also asked for a job.

The appearance of the brokers in the meeting with the female MP described above is of further interest. The use of brokers, or important people, was common in the past when constituents went to see their MPs. It was believed that when someone went to see an important person, such as the member of parliament, it would help if they were accompanied by a person of some stature in their village or community. In return for accompanying the constituent, the "broker" might expect a small gift; a bottle of arrack[7], a meal or some cash.[8] This once again reflected the personal nature of the ruler-ruled relationship in Sri Lanka. Assistance from a man of power was best obtained if one could show that he was a loyal supporter and friend of the ruler. The use of brokers fell into disrepute because many believed it was a corrupt institution. Most of the members, including the MP where the brokers were observed, stated that they would not allow brokers to enter their meetings. One member spoke of the brokers and how they operate. For a fee they would accompany their client and advocate the client's case before the MP, but as soon as the client left, the broker would relate the case realistically and usually tell the MP to ignore the client. In other cases the brokers would, in return for helping constituents, expect them to accompany the broker as an ad hoc group of villagers seeking a new road or irrigation channel. A group of ten to fifteen villagers would come and appear to represent the village involved. However, in many cases the new road or irrigation canal would benefit only one person, the broker. The villagers would come because they owed it to him or because it gave them the chance to meet with the MP and to promote their own personal need before the member of parliament.

The brokers observed in the meeting with the MP were both involved in local party politics and were officials of local party branches in the member's electorate. Before many of the petitioners arrived, they sat around the desk of the MP and chatted about party politics and told the MP of people in the party who were working behind her back to discredit her. After the crowd had begun to gather, they stood milling at the fringes of the crowd in the meeting hall chatting with friends. In a short time they began accompanying people to her desk and introducing them to her. In some cases, friends would come up to them and introduce them to an acquaintance. They would then talk to the newly met person to find out what they wanted, and sometimes after what appeared to be bargaining, they would accompany the person to the desk of the MP. It should be noted that the brokers did not appear to be seeking monetary gain but rather appeared to relish the idea of having access to power and the exercise of that access. They may have been establishing a base of influence if they ever sought higher position in the party. They appeared to behave more like campaigners rather than bribe takers.

Several studies of local Sri Lankan politics have indicated that local leaders take on the role of a power broker in their community. (Wanigaratne, 1976:21; Perera and Krause, 1977:23). Access to an MP or any other important government official is seen as both a way to gain favor with the villagers and from the perspective of the villagers as a qualification for supporting the individual.

Thus it would appear that the Sri Lankan legislators make strong attempts to respond to the particularized demands of their constituents. As already noted, they made every effort to allow them to come to them by setting aside times to meet with constituents. However, the large number of demands for jobs resulted in far more people looking for jobs than could be accommodated. The ability of legislators to provide jobs was a function of the power and influence that they wielded in the government. As would be expected, backbenchers received far fewer jobs to distribute than did ministers.

Many members expressed frustration about being unable to respond adequately to the demands for jobs. In some cases, the frustration turned into anger over the large numbers coming and demanding jobs. These attitudes are discussed in the last section of this chapter.

The job situation was further complicated by the high expectations of the Sri Lankan young people who often desire white collar jobs. Many were not willing to accept employment as manual laborers. As a result of this, labor shortages have existed in some areas. This was especially the case in those parts of the island where large-scale irrigation projects were being undertaken. An example of this can be found at a factory of the Ceylon Ceramics Corporation where several vacancies could not be filled. The corporation had selected thirty-two applicants whose names had been supplied by the government. Only eight of these accepted the job and of these eight, only two finally showed up for work (Ceylon Daily News, May 4, 1979).

In the Eighth Parliament, the government made two attempts to reduce the role of MPs in distributing jobs. The first of these came with the promulgation of the constitution of 1978. The new constitution included provisions to abolish the single-member electoral districts and replace them with several multi-member districts with seats determined on the basis of proportional representation.[9] Thus at the outset of this study in September, 1978, there were no single-member electoral constituencies in the country. However, the change to proportional representation had not yet affected the nature of the legislator-constituent relationship as the constituents still flocked to the MP who had been elected to represent them in the elections of 1977. Many MPs stated that the changes would lead to disaster, as the constituents would be left without a personal representative to attend to their needs. In any case, it appeared likely that the system of single-member electoral districts would continue in practice until the next elections scheduled for 1989,[10] even though they had been formally discontinued with the promulgation of the new constitution.

The second attempt to limit the demands placed on the legislators initially appeared to have more immediate potential to attack the problem. This was the creation of a "job bank." The job bank, instituted in March, 1978, was created to fill "all job vacancies in the public, local government and corporation sector where the particular job carries a salary of not more than rs. 850/per month"[11] (Weerasooria, 1978). All vacancies were by law to be filled through the job bank. Potential job seekers were given job bank applications which once filled out and accepted were placed into a computer which would then make selections on the basis of merit. Appointments were to be made to all regardless of their political affiliation (Sun, June 7, 1979). In practice the scheme has not worked as planned but appears to be a continuation of the old system. To become registered with the job bank, one must receive job bank forms. The number of these forms available was limited and most were distributed by the government members of parliament who gave them to their supporters. In addition, the members of the SLFP did not receive the forms to distribute while, in some electorates controlled by the opposition parties, the electorate's UNP party organizer received the forms for distribution. In addition, it was possible to circumvent the system. Job seekers could be appointed to jobs and then be given applications to the "job bank" after their appointment. This was done shortly before the May 1979 Urban and Municipal council elections in areas where the governing party, the UNP, wanted to make a strong showing such as the Jaffna peninsula.[12]

Although the job bank system was new at the time of the interviews, it appeared to have serious difficulties. At the time the interviews for this study were made, it still did not have any impact on the behavior of the legislators. In some cases, the members involved had given all of the forms they had received to their local party branches to distribute and thus had tried to remove themselves from the job placement functions of their work as an MP. However, most MPs were still involved in the distribution of jobs in their electorate because they perceived local party leaders to be corrupt and in need of supervision. Thus, the constituents were still coming to them. Since the interviews were conducted the job bank does not appear to have been any more successful. Every year during the budget debates both government and opposition members have severely criticised its operation. It would appear from the content of these debates, patronage and political pressure are still important in obtaining government employment, even through the job bank.

An additional problem arising from the intense pressure for jobs has been the question of bribery. Since the defeat of the SLFP in the elections of 1977, there have been a large number of allegations of bribery against some of the members of the SLFP. It would appear that the members of the Eighth Parliament are not free of corruption either. One member from Galle district in the south has been removed from parliament and several others have been forced to resign because of allegations of corruption against them. The most flagrant form of bribery is the selling of jobs.[13] Informal conversations with constituents found that many spoke of job selling by the MPs. In addition, the prices of jobs were common knowledge among the constituents and the going rates were frequently high.[14]

The causes of job selling arise from two problems. The first, possibly least important is the low salary of Sri Lankan MPs. Their monthly salary in 1979 was one thousand rupees[15] while the fringe benefits were relatively limited. However, the main problem behind the corruption appeared to rest in the cultural attitudes and traditions of the people. One Communist Party MP[16] stated that "The South Asian sense of bribery is different. When people go for a favor, they always bring something for the person doing the favor. It is just politeness. This carries over to politics. I said no to them but you can't refuse them without hurting them." A government commission report shortly after independence stated that "there is no doubt that the giving of gifts to a person in authority is ingrained in our customs and traditions" (Government of Sri Lanka [Ceylon], 1949:65). The establishment of western institutions created a situation where the traditional forms of politeness took on sinister meanings. The MP faced with receiving a small gift in response to small favors, was now doing very big favors for parents of children who saw their children educated but unemployed. The temptation exists to expect money or something of value. The villagers feel the cultural need to provide their benefactor with something to show their appreciation. Thus a system develops where "corruption" can run out of control. In western societies, the tradition of offering campaign gifts for favors by legislators has become highly institutionalized and accepted in the eyes of the law and the voters. In Sri Lanka, the cost of election campaigns is quite low and there is no need for candidates to solicit funds. Thus, the unemployment situation and the pressure for jobs on the legislators creates a situation where there are no legal and acceptable ways of repaying favors. This is not to say that a large number of MPs were corrupt but only to indicate that pressures existed which made corruption possible, especially in light of the lack of institutions to "legalize" the repaying of favors by the constituents.

As noted in Chapter 3, a majority of the members stated that meeting with constituents for particularized benefits was the main use of their time but very few of them felt that it was the most important part of their job. Each member was asked whether they felt that meeting with their constituents was a burden. Almost one-half expressed varying degrees of dislike of the job. Only five members stated that they enjoyed or liked meeting with their constituents (see Table 5.6). Forty stated that they disliked it or expressed their negative feelings in more colorful terms such as "disgusting," or "you become a glorified peon." In between these two extremes were a large number of MPs who either expressed neutral opinions or mixed emotions about the state of affairs. This latter group of about sixteen members stated that it was a burden, hard and wasteful but that "it is the duty of the job. We must help."

Further analysis indicates that there are distinct differences between the levels of authority and

TABLE 5.6
Legislators' attitudes about meetings with constituents

Responses	Seventh		Eighth		Total	
	no.	percent	no.	percent	no.	percent
Positive	1	2.2	4	10.0	5	5.8
Neutral or Mixed	13	28.3	27	67.5	40	46.5
Negative	32	69.6	9	13.5	41	47.7

TABLE 5.7
Legislators' attitudes about meetings with constituents and formal authority

	Seventh Parliament			Eighth Parliament		
	Positive	Neutral or Mixed	Negative	Positive	Neutral or Mixed	Negative
Backbenchers	0	4	22	2	7	2
Deputy Ministers	1	2	5	2	3	3
Ministers	0	3	4	0	7	3
Opposition	0	4	1	0	10	1
Total	1	13	32	4	27	9

Note: The Chi square value for the Seventh Parliament is equal to 13.8 with 4 degrees of freedom, significant at the .01 level while for the Eighth Parliament it is equal to 8.7, significant at the .01 level.

legislator attitudes toward the job (see Table 5.7). The opposition members expressed very few negative feelings about their role in dispensing particularized benefits. What is surprising is that when the results for the two parliaments are combined, the ministers expressed the most positive and the backbenchers the most negative attitudes among the government party members. It had been expected that the ministers would be the most negative because they had the most people coming to them. However when the number of constituents coming to the members is examined, there appears to be no relationship between the number of constituents coming to the members and their attitudes about their role in answering their demands (see Table 5.8). Even when the formal authority of the members was held constant,

TABLE 5.8
Average number of constituents coming to meet with MPs per week and attitudes about their role in meeting with them

	Number of MPs	Average
Positive	5	638.0
Neutral or Mixed	40	421.5
Negative	40	522.9

no relationship was found.

It does not appear that the number of constituents coming to meet with an MP affects his or her attitudes about the job. The ministers meet with the most people and yet have the most positive attitudes of the government members. The small percentage of negative attitudes expressed by the opposition members, however, appears to be the result of the number of people coming to meet with them. They receive so few demands that they do not feel burdened by them. The government members are so inundated by demands and the pressure that accompanies them, that the actual numbers coming does not necessarily affect their attitudes. Whether they are ministers or backbenchers, they receive too many demands for particularized benefits.

The ministers may find dealing with their constituents easier than the backbenchers find it because of the power and status attached to the post of minister. All ministers have extensive staff help so that much of the paper work involved in particularized benefits is taken care of by staff members. Most of the backbenchers have to do part of the paper work themselves. In addition, most of the ministers live outside of their electorates and only travel to their electorates on the weekends. Since most of the ministers refuse to meet with their constituents while in Colombo, it means that they only have to deal with particularized benefits a couple of days a week. The backbenchers, on the other hand, find their constituents gathering at their house as soon as the sun begins to rise. Thus, the numbers of constituents coming is not the crucial factor but perhaps the environment that one has to work in and the conditions that one finds in that work shapes the attitudes of the legislators. In the case of the ministers, the conditions and environment are much more conducive to doing the job.

Another factor affecting the attitudes of the legislators toward their role in the granting of particularized benefits may have been the timing of the interviews. Most of the members of the Seventh Parliament had suffered defeat in the general elections of 1977. This defeat, coming after seven years of trying to help their constituents in their personal needs, may have embittered them. Table 5.7 reports a distinct difference between the two parliaments in the attitudes of the members toward their role in granting particularized benefits. The Seventh Parliament members are much more negative about their role. They had spent seven years finding jobs for the long lines of constituents coming to them and then had been rejected by the same constituents at the next general elections. A general attitude of bitterness pervaded their interviews. Most said that giving jobs was useless and damaging. "If you give one member of a family a job and fail to give the rest a job, they all vote against you." Another stated:

> A man from a poor fishing family came to me looking for a job. I got him one as a cooperative rural bank clerk. Then he came to me and wanted to join the government clerical service. I found him a job. Later he came and wanted a transfer to Colombo. Then he wants a job for his wife. Then he hears there are six bank jobs. He wants one because it has higher pay. In the end he supported my opponent.

The members of the Eighth Parliament had very positive feelings about helping their constituents. "They are so grateful for what we do." "There is no greater satisfaction than making them happy."

Some of this difference may be explained by the relative newness of the Eighth Parliament members. At the time they were interviewed, most of the Eighth Parliament members had been in power for less than two years and did not have the memories of seven years of drudgery endured by the members of the Seventh Parliament. Most appeared to believe that their government would take care of the job problem and thus the numbers of youths coming to them for jobs would soon be declining.

This chapter has argued that there has been a sharp rise in the number of particularized demands placed on the Sri Lankan MPs and that this rise is the result of external factors in the society and economy of Sri Lanka. In addition, the number of demands placed on the MPs are a function of their formal authority. The responses to these demands and their attitudes about their job are also affected by the formal authority of the member. The next chapter examines the law making component of the legislator's job in Sri Lanka.

The significant point is that the citizens of Sri Lanka have used the ease of access to the MPs as a means to resolve personal and family problems. In response, the MPs have accepted this role, even if begrudgingly, by meeting with the voters and attempting to fill their requests. These constituent expectations and behavior are an important part of the interactive relationship discussed in Chapter 1, and as is argued in Chapter 9, a significant part of the success of stable democratic government in Sri Lanka.

NOTES

1. The currency of Sri Lanka is the rupee. At the time of the study it was worth approximately six United States cents.

2. Another source (Karunatilake, 1975:203) lists total welfare expenditures in 1960/61 as 651 million rupees and the 1974 expenditures as 1,644 million rupees. In 1949/50 he lists the total expenditures as 174 million. In either case the increase has been quite large.

3. The ministries which presented the most bills to parliament, and thus are the most influential in policy making are listed in Chapter 6. For additional information on them see Tables 6.1 and 6.2

4. According to Barker and Rush (1970:174) less than 10 percent of the British MPs receive more than one hundred letters a week. Puri (1978:259) reports the receipt of very few letters by Rajasthani legislators.

5. Telephone service in Sri Lanka is of questionable quality. This is especially the case with long distance calls from a member's constituency to Colombo. A caller must wait for an open line. The ministers are able to reserve a line.

6. The member involved had noted in an interview two weeks before the meeting was observed that the young women who come to see her always come alone.

7. Arrack is a locally brewed whisky made from the sap of the coconut palm.

8. In reviewing this manuscript A.J. Wilson noted that an occasional broker "would tell their client that the MP or minister needed money for the job to be done, and pocket the money" after receiving it.

9. For a description of the impact of this system of proportional representation see Oberst (1984).

10. The parliamentary elections originally scheduled for 1983 were postponed by the national referendum of 1982 until 1989.

11. This was approximately fifty-seven United States dollars.

12. Information provided by the UNP organizer of the area who seemed to be quite proud of his accomplishment in bypassing the job bank system.

13. At least 2 UNP MPs have been implicated in other types of corruption such as smuggling. Anura Daniel, former MP for Hewaheta was found guilty of smuggling 13 million rupees of gold, 540 watch movements and 158 pieces of garments from Singapore to Sri Lanka in 1982 (The Island September 28, 1984).

14. A 1959 commission investigating corruption among members

of parliament found that a large number of sub-postmasters were appointed after paying a bribe of 2,500 rupees each for the position (Government of Sri Lanka [Ceylon], 1960:56-66). During the period of the study, highly coveted positions such as teaching posts cost in excess of 5,000 rupees.

15. This was approximately sixty-seven United States dollars.

16. All of the Communist Party members interviewed made strong pleas for higher salaries. They claimed that a member could not live on the salary and that this forced members to take bribes. It should be noted that despite the widespread allegations of corruption against members of the 1970 coalition government, no Communist Party MPs have been accused. The member quoted above maintained his law practice while in parliament in order to have an adequate income.

6
Law-Making and Representation

This chapter examines the law-making process in Sri Lanka with special emphasis on the forces that influence the process and how the process is used by the members to accomplish their goals. It will be argued that law-making powers are concentrated among the cabinet members, with the backbenchers largely excluded although not completely devoid of power. The power structure of parliament influences the behavior of the legislators. In the highly structured nature of the law-making process, those members excluded from policy making attempt to use the institution to achieve other ends.

When asked what part of their job was the most important, almost 47 percent of the members stated ministry work, national legislation or the advocacy of national issues. Among these were over 80 percent of the ministers and 75 percent of the deputy ministers. The law-making function of legislatures is considered to be the main reason that legislatures were originally created (Blondel, 1973:11). Although the general trend in legislatures in other countries has been for a decline in their power over law-making (Blondel, 1973: Chapter 1), the Sri Lankan Parliament continues to have a significant role in the creation and enactment of laws.[1]

Law-making in Sri Lanka is centered around the cabinet but several other bodies in the parliament have the power to modify and change legislation. These are the government parliamentary group, consultative committees, and the sittings of parliament.[2] Each of these is discussed in this chapter.

As noted in Chapter 4, Sri Lankan legislators receive very few individual demands concerning their law-making activities. When constituents or others do make demands on national issues and legislation, it is done through organizations, and in the case of constituency based groups, they only appear to apply pressure when an issue of major importance arises. The only members feeling pressure over national issues are the cabinet ministers and even this pressure is limited. The rest of the members are exposed only to demands of a local nature.

The cabinet is the center of the law-making process in the Sri Lankan parliament. Under the Constitution of 1978, it is "collectively responsible and answerable to Parliament" (Government of Sri Lanka, 1978:30, article 43). Parliament technically has the "power to make laws,...and repeal...or amend...any provision of the constitution, or add any provision to the constitution..." (Government of Sri Lanka, 1978:48, Article 75). This power is tempered by the cabinet's control over almost all bills presented to parliament.[3] Once a bill is read before parliament, the cabinet relies on a strict code of party discipline within the legislative majority to enact the legislation. Thus, it is very rare that parliament will not pass a bill submitted to it by the cabinet. However, on rare occasions a bill may be abandoned by the government or amended.

Members of two cabinets representing the Seventh and Eighth Parliaments were interviewed for this study. Almost all legislation originated in the cabinet. The few bills which did not originate in the cabinet--private member's bills--required the approval of the governing party if one of their members presented the bill. Thus, many of the private member's bills were indirectly controlled by the cabinet.

In both parliaments, the policy making power of the cabinet was characterized by a concentration of power in the hands of a few cabinet ministers. This was especially evident in the Eighth Parliament. In that parliament, several ministers stated that there was very little debate on the cabinet papers presented to it and that it was very rare for a cabinet paper to be defeated. Before a cabinet paper was presented, very little discussion would occur between the ministers unless they directly involved in the legislation or the president organized the meeting. Thus the cabinet paper was a product of one ministry with consultation by the president. Since very few cabinet papers were ever defeated, most cabinet members' input into legislation was limited to minor amendments at the cabinet meeting.

In the Seventh Parliament, the situation was slightly different. It appeared that the policy making power of the SLFP government was also concentrated in the hands of a few ministers. However, as the cabinet of a coalition government, it was forced to reconcile the demands of all coalition partners as well as those of the SLFP ministers. This was made more difficult by the existence of several ministers who entered the cabinet with a base of support that was independent of their party. The CP and LSSP members of the cabinet, who represented a minority opinion within the group sought to use the cabinet as a deliberative body and turn the cabinet meetings into debates. By being better prepared, they felt that they could gain more influence than would have been expected on the basis of their numerical strength. Thus, although there was a tendency for power in the cabinet to gravitate to a few important SLFP ministers, the left parties struggled to spread the power among the members. This lasted until the LSSP was forced out of the cabinet in 1975.

An indication of the concentration of policy making power in the cabinet can be seen in Tables 6.1 and 6.2. The two tables report the number of bills introduced to parliament during two time periods, one in the Seventh and one in the Eighth Parliament. In both parliaments, a small handful of ministers presented a great majority of the bills. In the Eighth Parliament (see Table 6.1), four ministers presented almost two-thirds of the bills introduced during the period studied while almost one-half of the ministers did not introduce any bills. In the Seventh Parliament, three ministers presented over one-half of the bills to parliament while six of the remaining eighteen ministers presented no bills at all.

TABLE 6.1
Number of bills introduced by ministries from September 1978 to July 1979

Ministry	Number of Bills
Prime Minister, Housing and Construction, and Local Government	13
Finance and Planning	12
Trade and Shipping	7
Labour	7
Lands and Land Development and Mahaveli Development	4
Justice	4
Health	3
Agricultural Development and Research	2
Parliamentary Affairs and Sports	2
Education	2
Plantation Industries	2
Industries and Scientific Affairs	1
Power and Highways, and Posts and Telecommunications	1
Twelve other ministries	0
TOTAL	60

Note: The ministries held by the president who is no longer a member of parliament are excluded. Two bills were presented on behalf of those ministries by the prime minister and are included in his total.

TABLE 6.2
Number of bills introduced by ministers from June 1970 to November 1971

Ministry	Number of Bills
Finance	24
Public Administration, Local Government, and Home Affairs	10
Prime Minister, Defence, Planning, Employment and External Affairs	8
Foreign and Internal Trade	6
Plantation Industries and Constitutional Affairs	6
Agriculture and Lands	6
Labour	5
Transportation	3
Broadcasting and Information	3
Education	3
Industries and Scientific Affairs	2
Housing and Construction	2
Irrigation, Power and Highways	1
Shipping and Tourism	1
Justice	1
Six other ministers	0
TOTAL	81

A further indication of the use of the cabinet as a ratifying body for a small group of ministers, can be found in the responses of one of the ministers of the Eighth Parliament. He stated that, on the average, thirty items are brought up at each weekly meeting. Of these, 15 are over tenders on government contracts which are presented to the cabinet for approval, and the rest deal with cabinet papers and policy positions. Of the policy matters perhaps only two result in disagreement and have to be thrashed out. If the ministers are unable to come to a consensus, the president steps in and makes adjustments to satisfy all parties to the dispute. He could remember only one or two instances during his year in the cabinet where a vote had been taken.

After these thirty or so items have been discussed, the cabinet entertains any other matters that might be raised by the ministers. These are items that need immediate attention such as urgent foreign policy decisions or as was generally the case, urgent electoral needs such as a breakdown in the water supply of a village. These electoral needs may be transmitted to the minister directly or through the MP from the area in which the problem occurs.

Law-making power among the ministers is concentrated among a small handful of cabinet members. The decision making structure of the cabinet is centered around the head of the cabinet--the prime minister in the Seventh Parliament's cabinet and the president in the cabinet of the Eighth Parliament. The duties of the ministers who do not propose a large amount of legislation are concentrated in the administration of their ministries and only occasionally are involved in the making of laws.

It has been argued that the size of the cabinet in Sri Lanka is dictated by the need to represent "the numerous social, ethnic and religious groups" in the society in positions of authority (Wilson, 1974:195; also see Wriggins, 1960:98). It would appear that certain ministers are appointed to give representation to these groups while others are appointed to make the important policy decisions of the government. Thus, policy making power in the cabinet is limited to a few ministers and an apparent division exists between the policy makers in the cabinet and the other ministers. The deputy ministers have little input into the law-making process. They may sit in on cabinet meetings when the minister is out of the country or indisposed, but generally are not given the opportunity to present or prepare cabinet papers. Their only major input into the papers may come through informal discussions with their minister.

Before a bill is enacted into law by parliament, it is sent to several institutions which were created to provide law-making power to the non-cabinet members of parliament. The law-making power of these institutions and how they are used by the members will be discussed in the following sections.

PARLIAMENTARY GROUP

The government parliamentary group is made up of all MPs who support the governing party or coalition.[4] This in the past has included coalition partners, independents and appointed members. This group meets regularly prior to each meeting of parliament[5] to discuss the business before the assembly and to approve the legislative proposals of the cabinet. In practice, the group's influence is limited and dependent on the amount of power that the leaders of the cabinet are willing to give it. It has been noted that the group has: gone through periods in which it has accepted the power of the cabinet from 1948 to 1952 (Wilson, 1974:302); been provided a veto power over some legislation under the government of S.W.R.D. Bandaranaike from 1956 to 1959;

and been given the power to pass legislation under the governments of John Kotelawala from 1952 to 1956 and the first government of Sirimavo Bandaranaike from 1960 to 1954 (Wilson, 1966). Prime minister John Kotelawala was known to bring some issues to the parliamentary group before they went to the cabinet, while Sirimavo Bandaranaike during her first government would go to the parliamentary group on important matters before going to the cabinet (Wilson, 1966:18-19).[6] Another observer has noted that the parliamentary group of Dudley Senanayake's government from 1965 to 1970 "continued to play an active role" (Kearney, 1973:44-45). It is apparent that the parliamentary group's power has varied from parliament to parliament.

It would appear that there is a distinct difference between the use of the parliamentary group by the two parties. The SLFP appears to have permitted far more backbench input into law-making than has the more unified UNP. One observer of the Sri Lankan party system in the 1960s has written that

> almost every policy considered or presented by the cabinet or a minister involves a campaign among the backbencher constituents of the party [SLFP], and the decisions of an SLFP government are often the product of a primary election held among its own members (Woodward, 1969:196).

Of the UNP he has written that "policy is still primarily a function of the leadership." It is clear that the parliamentary group of the Seventh Parliament had more influence over policy than does the group in the Eighth Parliament. Nevertheless, both groups had limited control over their government's policy.

The government parliamentary groups of the two parliaments studied here were part of two distinctively different governments. The government of Sirimavo Bandaranaike was a coalition government and constantly had to accomodate two ideological factions within it. Both the left and right factions had their supporters in the cabinet and both groups attempted to use the parliamentary group to win their case. In the Eighth Parliament, the government of J.R. Jayawardene has been highly unified on policy matters and little dissension appears to exist.[7] Under these conditions, the parliamentary group of the Seventh Parliament had more policy influence than did the group in the Eighth Parliament.

Despite the differences between the two parliaments, the members of both were generally critical of their role and influence in the group meetings. It was apparent from the members of both groups that the purpose of the group meetings was not to create policy but rather as one member stated "to protect the government."

The group was used to prevent the appearance of open criticism. "The group meetings take care of disagreements and problems. The cabinet minister can know what the problems of the MPs are and their thinking on the issues...This gives the prime minister and cabinet an idea of their thinking." The doctrine of collective responsibility in the cabinet is carried over to the backbenchers in a doctrine of party responsibility and obedience. Disagreement with government policies must not come out in the open. The group meetings were used to give the cabinet a feeling of how the backbenchers felt about their decisions and allow them to criticise them in private before they might burst out into public view.

Most members felt that the legislative proposals put before them had already been decided upon and all that the cabinet sought from them was a rubber stamp of approval. If they had any influence on the final shape of the legislation it was on minor amendments and changes. However a significant bloc within the parliamentary group of the Seventh Parliament believed that they had a veto power over some legislation. This group consisted of several of the left party members and a group of SLFP members. Most of the "rebel" members interviewed for this study were part of this bloc. One member stated "At the parliamentary group meetings, I had little voice but I was known as a trouble maker. A group of us had some influence. We dominated the group by pretending to be thugs. We were very boisterous and threatening."

The success of the bloc was described by another member of the group.

> We had a pressure group of sixteen or so. Our first confrontation was to make the government accept the principle that property be nationalized. To make it more forceful, we met in Ratnapura[8] with forty or so MPs and deputy ministers.[9] We pressured until they accepted the principle. The second confrontation came when the cabinet proposed to cut the rice ration in the first budget to one measure. We suggested that they keep to the goal of national democracy and give power to the people and follow a socialist path. If this was done anti-capitalist sacrifices must be taken. We assembled a petition by 70 members saying that they would oppose the measure.
>
> The Cabinet held a midnight meeting and went back on the proposal.

The power of the bloc of members was only a veto power. "We could stop legislation but we could not get what we wanted." The power to shape legislation rested in the cabinet. The parliamentary group of the Seventh Parliament could add minor amendments or veto proposals but could not create or shape legislation to any large extent. In the end the rebels became frustrated and disillusioned. "I criticised a lot but nothing was ever taken up from it." "I stopped going, they [the parliamentary group] served no purpose, the power was in the cabinet."

In the Eighth Parliament, the group has been much more docile. Very little disagreement has arisen except on minor amendments and changes. Several members stated that they felt that they could not criticise because of the clauses in the new constitution creating a system of proportional representation. Under it, a member would have to rely on the party leaders to determine his position on the party's list of candidates in the next election. If they were highly critical, it was believed that they would appear lower on the list and thus might not be re-elected. An indication of the lack of debate in the group meetings came from one of the ministers who stated that the ministers rarely speak in the parliamentary group meetings.[10]

Although the parliamentary group meetings do not provide policy making opportunities for the backbenchers, they did serve another purpose; the advocacy of constituency needs (See Wiswa Warnapala, 1974:319). Sometimes these needs involve national policy matters as in the following example:

> During the food crisis, the government decided to allow higher food rations to urban areas. Now my area and the rural coastal electorates were worse off than the urban areas. I made a fuss over this and was able to convince the prime minister to give equally to all.

Other needs were more localized in nature and dealt with a single electorate. One backbencher stated: "Two weeks ago the meeting was held. I discovered that some people were given jobs illegally and took action to stop it including discussing it at the parliamentary group meeting." It would appear that particularized demands not resolved by a minister eventually find their way to the group meetings.

The backbenchers appear to have little input into the legislative process through the group meetings and what influence they do have is limited to certain areas such as the veto power discussed earlier and the minor amendments that can be added to legislation. The meetings do, however, provide a rare opportunity to express their feelings on pending legislation. Even when Wilson's observations (Wilson, 1966), mentioned earlier, about the influence of the group are considered, it appears hard to believe that the power of the group has ever been stronger than it was during the Seventh Parliament. The belief, stated by several scholars, that the group plays an important role in legislation and government policy making may be based on isolated instances of group influence rather than a pervasive and wide-spread influence over policy (Wilson, 1966:18; Kearney, 1973:44-46; Wiswa Warnapala, 1974:266-67).

The group, however, does play an important part in the creation of legislation as a testing ground for cabinet proposals. The cabinet can avoid the humiliation of defeat on the floor of parliament, and the even more costly dissension that might result from back-bench dissatisfaction by using the parliamentary group as a mechanism to vent disagreement on policy matters. However, it does not appear that the group takes an active role in policy making and the ability of the group to veto bad legislation may also be limited, especially to ideological or emotional issues where a bloc of members can generate enough support to block a bill at the group meeting. It does not appear that they have the power to stop bad policy unless the policy is ideological or highly emotional. An indication of this was provided by a minister in the Bandaranaike government of 1960-1965. Legislation was presented by a cabinet minister on a matter of education policy. According to the respondent, the bill was poorly created and poorly administered. Each of the members of the cabinet sat back knowing that the bill needed to be changed and waited for another minister to speak up rather than challenge the minister involved and risk alienating him. The result was that things went from bad to worse while the ministers sat "leaning back in their chairs staring at the ceiling and whistling to themselves, while the policy wreaked havoc." In this case, the parliamentary group did not stop the bill, even though the minister admitted that several members of the cabinet had felt that the policy was poorly designed. Thus the parliamentary group appears to be an appendage of the cabinet, created to protect the government and its cabinet. Little policy making power rests in the group and what does is limited in its application.

CONSULTATIVE COMMITTEES

Consultative committees were created in the 1960s to provide backbench input into the law-making process. Each ministry has a committee with the minister in charge of that ministry acting as chairperson of the committee. The system resembles the committee system

that existed under the Donoughmore Constitution
(1931-1948) where each ministry had its own committee
(see Namasivayam, 1950:95-104). However, under the
Donoughmore Constitution chairs were selected by the
members of the committee, and acted as minister. The
committees were instrumental in forming legislation.
However, the committee members used the committees to
further their own personal power and little cooperation
and coordination existed between the various committees
in the government. The system eventually fell into
disfavor. Under the Soulbury Constitution (1947-1972)
a similar committee system was not tried again until
after the 1956 elections when advisory committees were
set up (Kearney, 1973:46). The committees of the Sixth
Parliament (1965-1970) "proved to be of little lasting
significance" (Kearney, 1973:46) as did the committees
set up in the Seventh Parliament. The failure of the
ministers to provide the committees with any real power
resulted in infrequent meetings, and frustrated and
disillusioned members.

The committee system was reconstituted during the
Eighth Parliament and an attempt was made to create
them in the image of the United States Congress' committee system (Jayawardene, 1979). Interviews with the
members made it very clear that this had not been the
result. Only a handful stated that they had discussed
legislation during the committee meetings they had
attended. However, when asked whether the committees
were of any value, almost one-half of the backbenchers
gave positive responses. When asked why they felt the
way they did, none stated it was because of the policy
discussions of the committees. Most of the positive
responses were attributed to the usefulness of the committees in discussing administrative matters and local
needs (see Table 6.3).

Most of the members appeared to see the committees
as a means to redress constituency grievances and not
to shape policy. The weakness in the system results
from the power being left in the hands of the ministers.
They determine when and how often the meetings will be
held, the subject matter that will be discussed, and
have the final say over whether criticisms and suggestions will be acted upon. Several of the members complained that the meetings were held infrequently.
"They are called on the whims and fancies of the minister involved." Some met once or twice every two months
for an hour or so. The subject matter of the committee
meetings depended on the minister. Some ministers who
had presented several bills to parliament did not
discuss them with the committees, others notified the
committee of the bill shortly before it was to be presented to parliament. In only one case did a minister
make a concerted effort to obtain wide opinion on the
legislation being prepared in his ministry by asking

TABLE 6.3
Members' attitudes toward the consultative committees

	Total		Parties					
			UNP		SLFP		TULF	
	no.	per.	no.	per.	no.	per.	no.	per.
Positive reactions	10	47.6	5	62.5	0	0.0	5	55.6
For policy reasons	0	0.0	0	0.0	0	0.0	0	0.0
For administrative reasons	4	19.0	2	25.0	0	0.0	2	22.2
For electorate needs	6	28.6	3	37.5	0	0.0	3	33.3
Mixed or neutral reactions	6	28.6	3	37.5	3	75.0	0	0.0
Negative reactions	5	23.8	0	0.0	1	25.0	4	44.4
	21	100.0	8	100.0	4	100.0	9	100.0
Not assigned to a committee or no response	6		5		0		1	

opposition members not on the committee to come to the meeting in which the legislation was to be discussed. The responses of the ministers to the criticisms and suggestions offered to them also varied. Most of the members interviewed were unable to say whether their suggestions were acted on by the minister. In most cases, they felt the the minister listened and then ignored the suggestions. Several members of the Seventh Parliament held very negative attitudes towards their committees. The following quotation reflects this sentiment, "Some ministers, however, didn't like the criticism. Most ministers like to listen to secretaries[11] and directors rather than the people."

The impressions of the ministers concerning the committees were generally favorable. They stated that the committees gave them ideas, and an impression of how the opposition and backbenchers felt about the work of the ministry. They clearly saw the committees as advisory councils that could be approached when they felt it necessary. The district ministers apparently did not appear to value the committees and tended to their own business in their districts although one did state that he found that the committee meetings were useful because he could take up matters concerned with the development work in his district at the meetings.

The committees had one additional function, that of overseeing the administration of the ministries. Allegations of administrative failings or corruption can be presented before the committee and the accused parties can be forced to face their accusers and respond to them. In the same sense, government corporations and others dealing with government money can be required to present their records and defend their actions against anyone who might come to challenge them. One MP who had been a corporation head before coming to parliament reflected on his experiences before the committees: "I was called on to answer everything, not just finance. Also the minister must answer. Every year we had to come before the committees. It [the consultative committee system] was a much better accounting than before under the Public Accounts Committee."

The consultative committees did not appear to provide the members with much policy making power although the committees did serve other functions such as the advocacy of constituency needs, and the opportunity to meet face to face with a minister for help in resolving problems or offering advice. This may have been especially true for the opposition members who are excluded from the patronage network and often have difficulty reaching ministers for help. The relatively high number of opposition members who expressed positive feelings about the committee system may reflect the fulfillment of these needs. The committee system appears to provide one more opportunity for the backbench and opposition members to have input into the law-making process even if that opportunity is relatively limited.

FLOOR ACTIVITY

The floor of parliament is the site of the final debate on legislation along with two other institutions which have provided an opportunity for the members to have input into the law-making process. These are the question time and private members' motions. The results of most floor debates are predictable. A strong code of party loyalty exists in which the members of a party must vote the position taken by their party leadership. This includes not only voting as their party has directed but refraining from criticising the party's position during the debate. A party member who votes against the position risks the possibility of expulsion from the party, or a severe warning and possible exclusion from other party activities. The subtle implications are that the member may even seriously hinder his or her elevation to a leadership position in the party. The seriousness with which failure to obey party rules is taken is mirrored by the suspension of three members of the government parliamentary group in the Seventh Parliament for abstaining on a vote establishing a criminal justice commission in the 1970s. Although they were eventually allowed back into the group meetings, the warning against further actions was made quite explicit by their suspension.[12]

In general, the role of the opposition members on

the floor of parliament is quite limited. Most stated that it was a farce. They believed that its only purpose was as a forum to present their case and criticise the government. They had little hope of affecting legislation although several said that proposals that they had made in debate had been taken up by the minister involved.

Thus, much of the behavior on the floor of parliament is symbolic in nature. It is meant to project a certain image of the member to the world outside parliament. This may include, not only the member's constituents, but the international community as well. This was the case with the TULF members who hoped to expose their allegations of human rights violations by the Sinhalese against the Tamils to the international community. Other members often praise constituents by name during debates while some raise specific problems in their electorate that have been brought to their attention. Some members even print their parliamentary speeches and distribute them to their constituents. Others rely on the printed copies of the parliamentary debates to carry their message. Most members believe that there is wide interest in the debates and that they are read by a large number of their constituents.

Since the debates and the floor activities are mostly a ratifying exercise and not an instrument of policy making, an attempt will be made to analyse how they are used and the way in which they have been structured to meet the members' needs. The three elements to be examined will be the initial question and answer period at the beginning of the sitting of parliament, private member's motions which are not bound by the rules of party loyalty, and the floor debates on legislation.

QUESTION ASKING

The question time is an extremely important means for both opposition and backbench members to influence government behavior. Parliamentary meetings begin with the ministers or their deputy ministers answering questions posed by the members. The number of questions a member may ask is limited to three per meeting and must be submitted in advance. The minister then has the discretion to delay answering the question. An An additional question time occurs during the adjournment debate where matters of immediate urgency are supposed to be dealt with. These frequently involve allegations of political harassment against opposition members or localized emergencies.

Before analysing the question period and the question askers, it should be noted that question asking involves a great deal of strategy. The asker must clearly phrase the question so that the minister or deputy minister answering the question can not evade it. In addition, the ministers in charge frequently will ask for more time in order to delay giving the information to the opposition. Another delaying tactic is for a government member to plant a poorly worded question that will allow the answerer to avoid giving information and thus force the opposition to submit a new question which will delay their receipt of the information.

The question period reflects three types of demands: national, electorate or regional, and personal. In general, it is used by the opposition to obtain information, embarass the government or publicize the injustices and mistakes of the government.[13] The questions asked by the members from June 1970 to November 1971 during the Seventh Parliament, and from September 1978 to July 1979 during the Eighth Parliament were examined.[14] Several patterns existed in both parliaments. Question asking is done predominately by the opposition, although a relatively large number of questions are asked by the government backbenchers (see Table 6.4). No ministers or deputy ministers asked any questions during the periods studied. The rebels from the Seventh Parliament asked a disproportionate number of questions. The government coalition rebels asked forty-two questions or 25 percent of the total number of questions asked by government supporters. The opposition rebels asked 127 questions (44.4 percent of the total asked by the opposition). Both of these proportions exceed the percent that would be expected on the basis of their percentage in the group they come from.

An interesting feature of the question period is its domination by a small handful of members. In the Seventh Parliament, the top five question askers asked 257 questions or over 56 percent of the total number of questions. The average backbench or opposition member of parliament does not ask many questions. Most ask one or two questions a year.

The analysis of the content of the questions asked in both parliaments indicates that well over half of the questions related to constituency or regional matters (see Table 6.5). Although Table 6.5 shows a difference between the two parliaments in the focus of the questions asked, this difference is the result of one Seventh Parliament UNP member who asked over twenty-five percent of the total questions asked during the period under study. Over eighty-five percent of his questions dealt with personal matters. When he is dropped from the anlysis, the difference between the two parliaments is sharply reduced. In any case, the content of most of the questions deals with matters of importance to the questioner's constituency such as

TABLE 6.4
Questions asked by party

	Seventh Parliament June 1970 to November 1971			Eighth Parliament September 1978 to July 1979		
	Number of MPs	Questions Asked	Percent of Total	Number of MPs	Questions Asked	Percent of Total
UNP	17	201	44.3	141	41	15.8
SLFP	91	115	25.3	8	140	56.7
FP (TULF)	14	85	18.7	18	67	27.5
TC	2	5	1.1	*		
LSSP	19	13	2.9	*		
CP	6	9	2.0	*		
IND	2	26	5.7	*		
Total	151	454	100.0	167	248	100.0

*Party not represented in parliament.

TABLE 6.5
Focus of questions asked

	Seventh Parliament June 1970 to November 1971		Eighth Parliament September 1978 to July 1979		Total	
	No. of Questions	Percent	No. of Questions	Percent	No. of Ques.	Per.
National	144	31.7	132	53.2	276	39.3
Local	310	68.3	117	46.9	427	60.7
General	110	24.2	38	15.3	148	21.1
Particularized	188	41.4	59	23.8	247	35.1
Regional	12	2.6	20	8.1	32	4.6
Total	454		249		703	

individual requests for pension rights, back pay, or the job employment situation in general. Many of the nationally oriented questions also related to the employment situation. Many questioners dealt with policies on hiring and dismissing workers and asked for a complete list of the people hired and dismissed by a department in a ministry over a period that, in some cases, extended for several years.

There appeared to be little difference between the topics of the questions asked by the major parties. However, the content of the questions asked by the rebels in the Seventh Parliament did vary from the questions asked by the other members of parliament. They tended to ask more questions dealing with national issues than did the other MPs. This once again indicates their national orientation. An analysis of the ideological orientations of the question askers among those members interviewed indicated no difference in the content of the questions asked.

The members of the TULF and earlier the FP did show a difference in the type of questions they asked. Most of their questions concerned the language problems of the Tamil people. Many of their questions attempted to show how the Tamils were being discriminated against by the Sinhalese controlled government.

Thus question asking is a backbench and opposition activity which deals quite heavily with particularized and constituency matters. It does not have much effect on policy and is mainly used by the opposition parties to embarass the government with their questions about government policies and action.

PRIVATE MEMBER'S BILLS

Another means of backbench input into the legislative process is through the introduction of private members' bills. These are legislative proposals presented by individual members which are not bound by the usual confines of party loyalty. Each member is free to vote on the bill as they choose. However, a certain amount of scrutiny is exercised by the party of the member introducing a bill. The party generally must approve the bill before the member will be allowed to introduce. For example, in 1979 a backbencher announced to the press that he was planning to present a private member's bill to prohibit the advocacy of an independent Tamil state, a central tenet of the opposition TULF. There was an immediate outcry in the press and the bill was silently dropped after party leaders spoke to the member.[15]

Private members' bills are introduced relatively infrequently to parliament. During the eighteen month period analysed in the Seventh Parliament they were introduced at the rate of one every two months and in the nine month period in the Eighth Parliament at the rate of about two a month. During the two periods studied sixteen out of twenty-one bills were introduced by backbenchers, three by opposition members and two by deputy ministers.

The content of the bills tended to reflect the desires of the supporters of the member presenting the bill. A large number of the bills, eight, were religious in nature generally reflecting a minority religion's needs. Three others were oriented toward the member's constituency. However, several were intended to have national effects. Among these was a bill to make the Buddhist holy day--the poya day--a holiday, another to establish a new site for the capital of the country and yet another to reorganize a ministry. In one case, one of the "rebel" members presented a bill "To Pay Tribute To the SLFP Victory" after the United Front's victory in 1970. The debate on this bill droned on for a great length of time as the members attempted to extol the virtues of the winning coalition and point out the weakness and shortcomings of the defeated UNP government.

The small number of bills presented does not allow extensive analysis, however it does appear that the members presenting private members' bills tended to participate more than average in the question period reflecting a greater interest in parliamentary floor activities.

FLOOR DEBATES

Another area of backbench activity in parliament is the floor debates. The debates are largely controlled by the government party. Very few bills are presented by the opposition and only a handful of motions are made by them. Each party is allotted a certain amount of floor time and that party can then decide who can speak for their party and for how long. Obviously some members are denied the right while others are given preference. In addition, many interjections are made during the debate when a member wants to challenge a statement of the member holding the floor.

In an attempt to understand the workings of the floor debate, the amount of time each member spent debating was analysed. Since it would be hard to time the actual length of the speeches on the floor of parliament, another measure was used. Each debate is published in the _Parliamentary Debates (Hansard)_. The _Parliamentary Debates (Hansard)_ is divided into two columns a page. The number of columns in which a member's speeches appeared during the periods under study were noted and used as a measure of the amount of time spent debating by each member. The measure does include some inaccuracy in that a member speaking for only one line in the column would receive credit for speaking in one column, the same as a member whose speech took up the whole column. However, it is hoped that interruptions of this nature are random and the discrepancies will even out over time.

In general, the floor debate is dominated by the

ministers (see Table 6.6). They are the ones who present the bills and have the chief responsibility to defend them in parliament. The only chance that the backbench members have to participate actively in debates is during the budget debate in the fall of each year. Each ministry's appropriation is debated and the backbenchers if they want, may comment on them. However, their influence is extremely limited.

The average minister spends far more time debating than does the average backbencher or deputy minister. The data for the Seventh Parliament reveal that one deputy minister dominated the debate time of the deputy ministers. When he is dropped from the analysis, the average deputy minister's speeches in the Seventh Parliament appeared in 86.5 columns of debate during the period under study.

Among government members, the hierarchical structure of power appears once more. The ministers dominate the proceedings while the deputy ministers and backbenchers remain quietly on the benches. Even among the ministers a hierarchy can be seen. Those ministers who presented the most bills to parliament[16] tended to spend more time debating (see Table 6.7). This is natural since they are called upon to lead the debate on the floor of parliament. However, those ministers in both parliaments who did not present any bills to parliament averaged about the same number of columns as did the deputy ministers. The group of "rebel" members also continued to appear as they have in the other aspects of this analysis. The "rebels" averaged nearly as many columns debating as did the ministers (see Table 6.8). Once more, their actions appear similar to those of the ministers despite their status as backbenchers.

Other possible explanations in the variation in

TABLE 6.6
Average number of columns of debate and formal authority

	Seventh Parliament June 1970–Nov. 1971		Eighth Parliament Sept. 1978–July 1979	
	no.	ave.	no.	ave.
Opposition	30	178.1	25	145.0
Government ministers	19	211.5	25	114.4
Deputy ministers/ District ministers/ Non-cabinet ministers	19	119.1	52	29.9
Backbenchers	80	69.6	63	29.8

TABLE 6.7
Columns of debate and ministers divided by number of bills introduced to parliament

	Columns of debate			
Bills introduced	0-43	44-71	72-199	Above 199
0	8	5	3	0
1-2	2	3	3	2
3-5	1	1	4	1
More than 6	0	1	1	8

Note: Chi square is equal to 28.6, significant at the .001 level with 9 degrees of freedom. Gamma is equal to -.73.

TABLE 6.8
Average columns of debate with rebels and ministers divided by bills presented to parliament

	Seventh Parliament June 1970-November 1971		Eighth Parliament September 1978-July 1979	
	number	average	number	average
Active ministers	6	427.7	6	327.8
Other ministers	12	116.6	19	50.7
Deputy ministers	19	119.1	52	31.4
Backbenchers	72	57.3	63	32.6
Rebels	8	177.1	--	----

columns of debate do not explain as much as the hierarchy of power discussed above. Party differences within the 1970 coalition are not great although the leftist parties have slightly higher averages than do the SLFP and the other coalition members (the TC and 2 Independents). Nor does ideology or caste appear to be a factor in the variation among the members even within the groups of ministers, deputy ministers and backbenchers.

An analysis of ethnic groups is also limited by the small numbers of members involved. However, what data does exist, indicates that both the Moor and Tamil MPs whether they are ministers, deputy ministers, backbenchers, or opposition party members in the SLFP or UNP, spend less time debating (also see Oberst 1985a). It should be noted that the averages were not considerably lower among the Moor opposition members in 1970, and the Moor backbenchers in 1970 and 1977. It is very likely that these groups due to some unexplained cultural factors do not participate actively in the debates. Even among the Federal Party and TULF members, the average number of columns are lower than the average of the other opposition party. In 1977, the TULF leader was the leader of the opposition and thus would have had some control over the allocation of debating time and bearing the responsibility of leading the opposition to the government. Thus the evidence, however weak because of the sample size, indicates that the ethnic attachments of a member had a limited influence on the floor behavior of that member. However the number of Tamil and Moor members is relatively small and therefore does not play a major role in the determination of who will debate.

It would appear that the single most important factor in determining activity in floor debates is the formal authority of the member involved. Other factors such as caste and ethnicity may be a factor but are not a major determinant of debate activity.

The content of the debates by backbenchers indicates their strong advocacy of their electorates. The backbenchers receive their greatest opportunity to participate in debates during the budget debate. At this time they will frequently make a listing of their constituency's problems that relate to the ministry whose budget is being debated. In some cases the members bring up personal problems faced by some of their constituents and in others they may stress the needs of the ethnic group or caste community of which they are a member.

Thus the floor debates of the backbenchers are used to represent the localized needs of their electorates and more specifically their supporters. Although their speeches may, at times, deal with legislation, their prime objective appears to be the advocacy of their constituency's interests. An example of this may be seen in the maiden speech of an appointed member in the Seventh Parliament. Most of the "appointed" members were appointed to represent specific group interests as this quote will reveal. His speech comes from the debate on the throne speech outlining the government's program of policies.

> It is my privilege to represent the Roman Catholic interests in this Parliament.... This is the first time that the hand of friendship has been extended to us, and we readily accept this friendship and offer

> our wholehearted co-operation to this Government...
>
> I have also to state that in a way I represent another small minority community in this country, namely, the Bharata community....It is my privilege to pledge the loyalty of my small community to this government...
>
> Having discharged these two responsibilities, I must also state that I am the chief executive of a trading community....Having said my piece for my country, I think it is my duty to make an effective contribution in this House on behalf of the trade, commerce and industry of this country (Hansards vol. 90, 564-566).

Among the majority community members, the tendency is to represent their supporters in their electorates.

The analysis of the law-making process in Sri Lanka has indicated that most members are left out of the process and have little more than ratifying power over the legislation that is presented to parliament. They do not have the power to shape and form legislation beyond small amendments and changes to the context of the legislation. Thus law-making power is confined to the ministers and even among them there appears to be a hierarchy of influence with several influential ministers exerting disproportionate amounts of law-making power.

The mechanisms and institutions created to provide input into the law-making process for backbenchers and opposition members largely do not serve that function. They allow only for minor amendments and in some cases a veto power over unpopular legislation. The opportunities provided by the question period, the consultative committees, and to a lesser degree, the parliamentary group meetings are often used by the backbenchers to air grievances pertaining to their electorates. Even the time spent on debates frequently involves the problems and needs of the members' home electorates.

The Sri Lankan "law-makers" are largely excluded from making laws. Instead of making laws, they have turned the law-making process into a forum to present the needs of their electorates. In Chapter 4 it has been noted that the members received very little pressure from their constituents concerning laws that were pending before parliament or could potentially be presented to parliament. This chapter indicates that most members would have little power to effectively respond to any pressure for legislation. Law-making power rests in the hands of party leaders who receive that power because their party holds a majority of the seats in parliament. Individual MPs are not responsible for the policy choices taken by their party leaders. In Chapters 8 and 9, the significance of this finding is made clearer. Chapter 7 examines one additional area where the MPs have some ability to influence government actions--development work.

NOTES

1. Under the Constitution of 1978, the president has assumed many of the powers that had been held by the parliament. Wilson (1980:96) has argued that parliament "is no longer lonely in the splendid grandeur and eminence that" existed under the Constitution of 1972.
2. Informal structures do exist. These involve ad hoc groups of backbenchers going to the prime minister or president to petition him on a matter they feel that they can not get redress for, and informal meetings of the backbenchers and ministers.
3. A small number of private member's bills are submitted each year (this is discussed in a later section) and on occasion under the Soulbury Constitution of 1948 to 1972 motions of no confidence have been submitted by the opposition.
4. In the Seventh Parliament this included the members of the SLFP, the Communist Party, the LSSP, and the Tamil Congress. In the Eighth Parliament it includes the sole parliamentary member of the Ceylon Workers Congress as well as the members of the UNP.
5. Parliament sits twice a month, or more frequently if business necessitates.
6. This was clearly not the case in her second government from 1970 to 1977.
7. This, in part has been due to the changes incorporated in the 1978 constitution. Under the constitution, all seats of parliament belong to the party and the member sitting in that seat owes allegiance to the party. Thus a dissenting member can be replaced in parliament by one who will follow the party line.
8. A regional city east of Colombo.
9. The newspaper version of the meeting listed twelve MPs in attendance (Ceylon Daily News, August 13, 1970).
10. It should be noted that more criticism has appeared as the term of the parliament has progressed. However, many still feel reluctant to be critical.
11. The highest civil servants in a ministry are called permanent secretaries. The reference to "secretaries" refers to these officials and their asssitants.
12. Another example of this was the removal of the minister of Plantation Industries, M.D.H. Jayawardene from the cabinet for criticising the 1980 budget.
13. One long time Marxist who later became the Minister of Finance in 1970 has noted that the question time is the "most important" and "exciting" means of controlling the executive (Perera, 1964:21).

14. The two time periods selected are not of equal length. This is the result of the ministerial changes that accompanied the promulgation of the new Constitution in 1978. At that time and shortly after it, several deputy ministers were elevated to the post of minister while several backbenchers became deputy and district ministers. These extensive changes made it impossible to analyse the questions asked over the first eighteen months of the government as was done for the Seventh Parliament. As a result, the first nine months of the government under the new constitution were analysed.

15. In the fall of 1983 a similar resolution was introduced by the government and passed by parliament as the sixth amendment to the constitution. The resolution followed severe communal rioting during the summer of 1983. This reflects a sharp change of attitude between 1979 when the original proposal was suggested and 1983 when it was passed.

16. The active ministers in Table 6.8 are those who presented five or more bills during the periods studied. The others are those who submitted less than five.

7
Development Work

The role of legislators in the economic development process of Third World nations has generally been viewed in terms of policy output at the national level. Their role in development projects at the local level has rarely been studied. It is argued here and in the following chapters that the Sri Lankan legislator's role in development projects is a form of policy making that is of extreme significance to Third World political systems. Their actions are of significance because of the link they form between the national government and the needs of local villagers.

This chapter examines how allocations are divided under the system of the decentralized budget, the demands placed on the legislator for projects in his electorate, and the performance of the legislator in carrying out his or her projects. It is argued that the formal authority of a legislator has a smaller impact on his or her behavior in this component of the job than it does in the other components of the job. It is also argued that as in the constituency service component of the job, this component involves a great deal of interaction between the legislators and their constituents.

The legislator's involvement in rural development work is a relatively recent addition to the functions of legislators in Sri Lanka. Under a system introduced in 1973, all Sri Lankan legislators receive a block grant which they are free, within certain loose guidelines, to spend on development projects in their electorates. The legislator becomes the planner and administrator of the projects in his electorate. The plan is part of a broader attempt to decentralize development administration in Sri Lanka.

Prior to the advent of the decentralized budget, most members of parliament had little control over the development projects in their electorates. The money available for development projects was allocated to the various ministries involved and the minister in charge of the ministry had a great deal of discretionary power over how the money was to be spent. The ministers were in a position to deny money for projects in electorates controlled by opposition party members or in electorates held by potential challengers to the position of the ministers in their own party. In other words, the criteria involved could be very personal or political, or in some cases the minister could make the decisions on the merits of the projects. It would appear, from the general impression of the respondents, that most ministers made arbitrary judgments about who would receive funding for projects. In an earlier study by this author (Oberst, 1977), it was found that the allocation of money for irrigation projects under a five year plan in Sri Lanka was based on several arbitrary factors. Government party MPs, especially ministers, were favored in the allocation of monies. The influence that members of parliament had over the placement and choice of projects in their electorates was directly related to the relationship they had with the minister involved. A personal dispute with a minister could lead to a cutting off of funds for development projects. Several MPs complained that they did not even know about projects in their electorates until they were started. In some cases, they first learned of the projects when constituents came to them asking what was being built. Thus, the average backbench MPs had limited power over the development projects in their electorates.

From the time of independence until the 1970s, the government of Sri Lanka had seen a need for regional planning to foster rural development (Gamage, 1978). The early attempts failed and most authority over development projects remained in the central offices of the various departments of the ministries involved. In 1973, the United Front government attempted to set up a new system of rural development and planning. The scheme which will be referred to here as the decentralized budget (DCB) was initially centered around the district political authority (DPA). The DPA was a council comprised of the members of parliament from that district, the government agent of the district, and the local heads of departments in the district. A member of parliament was chosen as the political authority and acted as chairperson of the council.[1] Each DPA would receive a block grant of money and have the discretion to spend it on capital works in the district. Each MP on the council supposedly had an equal say over how the monies could be spent but in reality the "political authority" had the largest influence and in some districts actually dictated how the money would be allocated (Government of Sri Lanka, 1975:16, 23).

When the UNP came to power in July, 1977, the leaders attempted to reform the system and introduced what they called a "new" system, the district ministry scheme. It resembled the political authority system in every respect except that each electorate in a district was to receive an equal amount of money and that the district ministers were given clearly defined powers that had previously only been implied for the political authorities. Thus both systems were similar, a point agreed to by most of the MPs interviewed. Under the district political authority, the authority received a block grant for the whole district and decided how the money would be spent. The individual MPs would then receive allocations for new and continuing projects based on what the district political authority perceived as their need. Under the district ministry scheme, each electorate receives an equal amount for new projects while continuing projects are distributed on the basis of need.

This chapter examines the role of the MP in planning the use of these allocations and administering their expenditure. The role of the electorate and pressure groups is examined in each aspect of their actions. The first section looks at the receipt of the funds and how they are distributed among the MPs. This is followed by an examination of the forces affecting the choices taken by the MPs in allocating the money among the projects in their electorates. Section 3 explores the success of the MPs in completing the projects they plan.

DECENTRALIZED BUDGET ALLOCATIONS

As already mentioned, the system of allocating DCB funds varied between the two parliaments. Reference to the district political authority (DPA) will of course refer to the system of administering the decentralized budget during the Seventh Parliament while reference to the district ministry scheme will refer to the system under the Eighth Parliament. It should be noted that the projects under the decentralized budget were supposed to be used for capital expenditures although just what constituted a capital expenditure was frequently loosely defined. In addition, all money had to be spent before the end of the fiscal year (which is the same as the calendar year) or it would revert back to the central budget. Obviously, all projects could not be finished in one year and this necessitated a budget for projects continued from one year to the next. Of course, all of these "continuation projects," as they are called, had to be reapproved and a new allocation made. Thus, one finds two budgets under the system; a budget for new projects and one for continuing projects. The DPA or district ministry had to decide which projects required funding under both budgets. All projects had to be confined to one electorate. Anything larger was to be carried out under the capital budget of the department involved.

As with other aspects of a Sri Lankan MP's job, the formal authority of the legislator affected the way he or she functioned in the job. During the Seventh Parliament, the more powerful a member was, the greater the allocation the member received. This was especially true in the case of the political authority who in most districts received the largest share of the allocations. Many of the opposition MPs complained bitterly of the abuse of power carried out by the political authority. However, it should be noted that not all political authorities abused their privileges or were biased against opposition members. In some districts the opposition members claimed to receive equal shares of the allocations available. Variations in the government bookkeeping procedures between districts in Sri Lanka make the results of nationwide comparisons of electorates and expenditures questionable. Yet aggregate comparisons are of some value in pointing out general trends.

An attempt was made to gather data on allocations and expenditures in each electorate for each year of the budget (1974-79). In many cases the data was not available at all, or in a form which was not useful for the purposes of this study. The result is a patchwork quilt of electorates where data was available. In no year was a complete listing of allocations in all electorates available.

The analysis of the allocations in each electorate where data was available indicated that in each year (1974 to 1977) the political authorities averaged considerably higher allocations than did the other MPs. Table 7.1 reports these figures. It also indicates that in 1977, the political authorities received lower average allocations than did the ministers. This is a statistical illusion arising from a large number of ministers coming from one district which had very high average allocations for all members. In each of the five districts with political authorities where data was available, the political authority received higher average allocations than did the ministers. Because of high allocations in one district with a large number of ministers, the average allocations of all ministers appeared to be higher than the average allocations for the political authorities.

In two years, 1976 and 1977, the backbenchers averaged considerably lower allocations than did the deputy ministers and the ministers. The failure of a pattern to appear in the first two years, 1974 and 1975, may have resulted from an initial opposition to the DCB by many ministers. Some ministers felt that the plan would take away their power and discretion over development projects. Thus, it is possible that some backbenchers were able to get higher allocations because of

TABLE 7.1
Average Seventh Parliament DCB total allocations by party, formal authority and year

Party	1974 ave.	no.	1975 ave.	no.	1976 ave.	no.	1977 ave.	no.
SLFP								
Backbenchers	851.2	(23)	1327.6	(26)	2497.6	(37)	2385.1	(25)
Deputy ministers	671.2	(6)	1558.2	(5)	3542.6	(5)	2693.2	(4)
Ministers	592.6	(8)	1195.6	(10)	3647.3	(12)	3684.7	(3)
Political authorities	1770.5	(4)	2434.2	(4)	3833.1	(8)	2752.0	(5)
LSSP	241.6	(5)	379.6	(5)	2473.0	(9)	1565.3	(6)
CP	838.7	(3)	757.3	(3)	1519.5	(2)	1748.3	(3)
UNP	204.4	(5)	758.2	(8)	2318.5	(11)	1958.0	(5)
Tamil parties	-----		-----		931.0	(9)	1574.9	(9)
Total	743.9	(54)	1217.0	(61)	2639.3	(93)	2230.2	(64)

their greater interest in the DCB and the failure of some ministers to participate actively in the program.

Of interest in Table 7.1 is the failure of the left party coalition partners to receive allocations equal to the SLFP members in the government coalition. In the years before the LSSP left the government--1974 and 1975--the two Marxist parties in the coalition averaged considerably lower allocations than the other members. What is surprising is that the average for the LSSP increased sharply after they left the government coalition. This may reflect their party's initial opposition to the DCB while they were in the government[2] and their freedom to challenge and fight with the SLFP when it came time to allocate money for the budget after they left the coalition.

Even though the left parties received a smaller share of the allocations than did the other government MPs, they still fared better than the opposition parties. The UNP did very poorly in the allocation of funds in the early years of the budget, perhaps because most of their members came from urban electorates which did not receive as high an allocation as did the other electorates because of a belief that urban electorates needed less. In the later years, they received about as much as the LSSP members and in 1977 as much as the Federal Party members. The Federal Party members received very low allocations in 1976, although these figures may be incomplete and the average may be

misleading.
   In 1978, the system of allocating money under the decentralized budget was changed and the result was that each electorate received an equal amount of money in new allocations. However, this system did have some loopholes which permitted some members to receive higher allocations. The first was the tendency for MPs to pick up projects over the course of the fiscal year. For instance, if a member did not utilize his or her allocation, another MP might be able to take over the allocation of the funds. Thus it is possible for some members to receive more new allocations than others. No analysis of this loophole was made since the data were frequently not available. The second loophole was in the allocation of money for continuing projects. Here, there were no rules for distributing the money equally.
   The allocation of money for continuation projects was analyzed and the results indicated that the district ministers, as did the political authorities before them, received considerably higher allocations than did other members of parliament (see Table 7.2). However, among the other members of parliament there was much less variation in the allocation of funds than there was in the Seventh Parliament. In 1978, there was very little difference between the government members and the opposition members with the exception of the deputy ministers, who for some unexplained reason received far lower allocations. The equality in the distribution of allocations may have resulted from a late start in the system that year. Most members did not know how much money they would receive until a government memo three months after the start of the fiscal year directed that all continuation projects be funded. Thus there was little room for discretion and influence based on one's formal authority.

TABLE 7.2
Average Eighth Parliament continuing allocations by party, formal authority and year

Party		1978		1979	
		ave.	no.	ave.	no.
UNP					
	Backbenchers	1684.1	(45)	1620.8	(24)
	Deputy ministers	1218.0	(15)	1921.8	(13)
	Ministers	1741.4	(13)	1425.1	(7)
	District ministers	2406.7	(12)	2445.0	(12)
SLFP		1666.8	(4)	------	
TULF		1767.0	(4)	1042.8	(4)
Total		1713.0	(93)	1789.5	(60)

In 1979, the four TULF members, all from the East Coast, received far lower allocations than did the other MPs. The decline from their relative 1978 levels may have been the result of the UNP attempting, in the earlier year, to woo these members over to the UNP. These members were believed to be less committed to the TULF because of traditional differences between the Tamils on the Jaffna peninsula and those outside it.[3] It may have become apparent to the leaders of the UNP that these people would continue to support the TULF and attempts to appease them with extra allocations were discontinued. Unfortunately, data from Jaffna district were not available and thus, no attempt could be made to see whether the TULF members from the Jaffna peninsula received smaller allocations in both years.

Thus, the analysis of the distribution of allocations under the decentralized budget indicates that in its early years, 1974 to 1977, the distribution of allocations was biased in favor of those with formal authority in the parliament. Under the UNP government, a change has occurred in which the allocations are done on a much more equitable basis although the district ministers like their counterparts in the earlier government--the political authorities--still receive higher allocations for their electorates than do the others in their districts. In addition, the possibility that some opposition controlled electorates are not receiving a fair share of the allocations appears to exist although the data was not available to give conclusive evidence one way or the other.

THE FORCES AFFECTING THE MP'S PROJECT DECISION

Once the money has been received, the MP has complete control over how it will be spent within the guidelines of the district political authority's or district ministry's decision about the priority of the project. In the case of government members these guidelines can be circumvented, as is noted later in this chapter. In any case, the MPs' proposals are their own and how they come to make them varies a great deal between members. In some cases the members make the decisions solely on their own judgment, in others they set up committees to make the decisions about priorities to members of their staff or local government officials such as the assistant government agent. Thus the influence of the constituents on what projects would be funded varied from electorate to electorate. In addition, before a project could be approved by the district political authority or the district ministry, a feasibility study had to be done. (Once again this requirement varied in how strictly it was enforced.) The study had to be done by the technical branch of the department that would be doing the work. The members complained of delays by some of the departments and in some cases corruption related to getting the study done, but in general there were few problems connected with the studies for the government members. In the case of the opposition, the rules regarding the feasibility studies were enforced quite strictly. In addition, some opposition members complained that the bureaucratic redtape that permeates the Sri Lankan bureaucracy can be easily avoided by the government MPs but was unavoidable for some of the opposition MPs. One case deals with a TULF MP from the Jaffna peninsula who wanted to stock an inland lagoon with hatchlings to help create a commercial inland fisheries industry. The amount to be expended was relatively small, 1,000 rupees (US $67). He sent the proposal to the relevant department for a feasibility study which consisted of a cost-benefit analysis. The department ruled that the project was not feasible because there was no way to determine the value of the fish taken from the lagoon. The lagoon was quite large and the fishing going on in it was done by individuals for their own families or for markets in surrounding towns. Thus without being able to ascertain the benefits of the project, it could not be approved. Under normal circumstances government MPs could easily circumvent such a decision by exercising their influence, but opposition members are constrained because they have no power to threaten the bureaucracy or to reward it if it does what they want. The project was never carried out.

In order to understand the pressure that is exerted on the MPs concerning the selection and funding of projects, each member was asked how the decisions concerning the projects were made. Overwhelmingly, the members stated that they made the final decision (see Table 7.3). However, a significant but small number of MPs did set up committees which made the decisions (11.8 percent). Table 7.4 indicates that there was no difference between the formal positions of power in the parliament and the setting up of committees to evaluate the potential projects. Ministers were as likely to set up committees as were backbenchers. In most instances where a committee was formed, the MP of that electorate included himself or herself on the committee. Thus the importance and independent judgment of the committees may have been limited by the presence of the MP on the committee.

Since the MP controlled the decision as to what projects would be selected, it is important to find who, if anyone, they consulted concerning the projects. About one-fifth of the members stated that they consulted no one (22.6 percent, see Table 7.5). In most cases, these members were urban MPs who spent most of their decentralized budget on schools and school equipment, and

TABLE 7.3
Method of selection of projects under the DCB

	Number	Percent
MP	80	86.0
Committee	11	11.8
Clerk or government official	2	2.2
Total	93	100.0

TABLE 7.4
Formal authority and method of selection of projects under the DCB

	MP	Committee	Clerk/government official
Backbencher	31	5	0
Deputy minister	17	2	0
Minister	14	2	2
Opposition	18	2	0
Total	80	11	2

TABLE 7.5
Major organizations consulted by MPs

Groups	Percent	Number
Rural development societies	43.0	40
Local party branches	28.0	26
No groups consulted	22.6	21
Bureaucrats	19.4	18
Cultivation committees	15.1	14
Village councils	7.5	7
Prominent individuals	7.5	7
Parent-teacher associations	5.4	5
Total number of MPs		93

Note: Several MPs gave more than one answer.

thus claimed that they knew what was needed in their electorates or were rural members who had a long experience working in the electorate, and therefore "knew" what was needed in it. Several organizations were cited by substantial numbers of MPs. These were the rural development societies (43.0 percent), local political party branches (28.0 percent), and bureaucrats (19.4 percent).

The formal positions of power of the MPs appeared to be a strong indicator of the types of groups selected for consultation about the projects (see Table 7.6). The deputy ministers and ministers tended to make the decision themselves or rely on the advice of government bureaucrats while the backbenchers and opposition members relied on the local organizations for advice. This may have resulted from a greater sensitivity on the part of the backbenchers and opposition members to the needs of their constituents. The ministers and deputy ministers are preoccupied with their ministry work and may not be able to spend as much time on the projects and therefore either turn over some responsibility to bureaucrats or do not bother to take the time to consult any groups.

This is reflected in the proceedings of a seminar of government agents concerning the problems with the DCB held in 1978. Several government agents stated that the ministers and deputy ministers were very difficult to contact concerning their work and that they tended to be uncooperative (Government of Sri Lanka, 1979a:64, 139). In any case, the greater staff and financial resources available to the ministers and deputy ministers may be offset by the closer relationship that the backbenchers and deputy ministers have with the organizations in their constituencies.

The importance of local development organizations and their influence on the MP should not be underrated. The concept of local participation in development has permeated both parties and the result has been many

TABLE 7.6
Groups consulted and formal authority in parliament

	None	Bureaucrats	Local parties	RDS
Ministers	7	2	4	5
Deputy ministers	3	6	5	5
Backbenchers	6	8	17	20
Opposition	0	2	0	10

Note: $X^2=22.3$, significant at the .01 level of significance.

attempts to create representative rural organizations. Before examing their influence on the MPs, a brief description of the most important ones follows.

As mentioned earlier, the MPs consulted the rural development societies (RDS) about their development projects more frequently than any other organization. In addition, they were the most commonly cited organization that came to the MPs on other matters as well (see Chapter 4). The first rural development societies were formed in 1940 and by 1948 over three thousand societies had been established (Government of Sri Lanka, 1976:4). In 1952 the first women's society was started and by 1975 there were 384 Kantha Samiti or women's societies along with 3,789 rural development societies on the island (Government of Sri Lanka, 1976:22).

The societies were created to provide an opportunity for villagers to have input into the development projects in their village. Membership is open to all adults under the jurisdiction of a society which may encompass several villages. The success and activity of the organizations varies from society to society. As is noted later, much depends on the leaders of the organization involved. If the leaders do not take an interest in the society, it will in all likelihood be ineffective. In any case, the rural development societies play an integral part in the development work of most villages.

Local party organizations have existed more in name than in reality. In the first years after independence, one observer of Sri Lankan politics stated that "the candidate is the pivot of party organisation in a constituency" (Weerawardana, 1960:217). Much of party politics in Sri Lanka at that time involved personality oriented politics (Woodward, 1969:270). For the most part, local party organizations encompassed friends of the candidate running for office (Woodward, 1969:180). However, in the last two decades a shift has occurred in the importance of party organizations. As mentioned in Chapter 5, a pervasive patronage system has developed in Sri Lanka. This has fueled the development of party organizations and given them the rewards necessary to hold membership, exact volunteer work, and to have viable organizations. By 1970, the patronage system had developed sufficiently enough that the government parties were able, in some electorates, to establish effective local party organizations. It should be noted that both the LSSP and CP have had relatively effective local party organizations for many years (Woodward, 1969:214,216). It has been noted that even as early as the 1950s the LSSP local party organizations were heavily involved in rural development projects (Wriggins, 1960:139-40). Several SLFP members interviewed believed that a few of their MPs had established effective local organizations and that these were found among the younger MPs of the party while the older MPs tended to rely on personal loyalty for support. In the UNP, J. R. Jayawardene, the leader of the party, has made a strong effort to establish viable party organizations (see Wilson, 1974:136). The result has been that in some electorates, some functions of the legislator's job such as the job bank have been taken over by the local party branches. The local party branches of both parties are fueled by the patronage that the party in power can offer. Once the party is out of power as happened to the SLFP in 1977, the membership in the organizations declines and the organizations become inactive.[4] Yet, the local MP remains the most important influence in the party organization. Over 90 percent of the MPs interviewed stated that they had originally started the local party organization in their electorate.

An example of the dominance of the local MP can be seen in the case of a local party branch in the south of the country. The branch was formed on the instigation of the new MP one month after he was elected. Prior to his election, the electorate had been held by an MP who had been elected from the same party, but had crossed over to the opposition taking the local party organizations with him. The newly elected MP had requested that his supporters in the electorate form local organizations and hold meetings. The organizations remained active until the new MP also left his party and the branches fell into disuse.

In addition to the rural development societies and the local party branches there were several other organizations which have extensive influence over village life and were cited by the MPs. Included in this group were the cultivation committees, cooperatives, parent-teacher associations and various religious societies. As is noted later, the leadership in these organizations was frequently the same as the leadership in the RDS and party branches.

Thus the MPs meet with the leadership of these organizations and react in some way to their pressure. However, the leadership of these groups promotes very narrow interests. It is argued that the rank and file members of the groups have little input into the actions of the groups largely because of a lack of participation by the rank and file and domination of the organization by the elite of the village. This means that the groups effectively represent the interests of the leaders who come from a narrow elite in the villages. Despite the large number of rural development organizations in the villages, most of the organizations are led by the same people who are elected to office in the organization because of their influence in the village and their ability to deal with the local MP.

One study of the rural development societies

(Government of Sri Lanka, 1976:230) has indicated that only 12.2 percent of the eligible population in the areas covered by the societies have become members of the societies. Another study of a single village indicated that about 22 percent of the household heads in the village attend some special interest group meetings (Ryan, 1958:55). However, a study by the Rural Development Training Institute (Government of Sri Lanka, 1976) estimated that over half of the families in the areas encompassed by the societies had members in the societies. Thus, it would appear that membership in the societies is rather limited. Yet the real weakness in the input of the average member comes from their lack of participation in the activities of the organization.

Most societies rely on one or two members to carry out the activities of the organization. If these people lose interest, the organization frequently becomes inactive. The decline and inactivity of organizations has been noted in several studies (Ryan, 1958:150-51; Government of Sri Lanka, 1976; Gajanayake, n.d.:27-28). A very small group of people are active in the organizations. One study (Gajanayake, n.d.:32-33) found no evidence of low caste villagers being involved in the activities of the RDS in the village studied. In any case, attendance at most meetings is quite low. This has been found by Ryan (1958:154) and in a local party organization observed for this study where attendance was relatively large in the first few meetings but soon dropped to seven or eight members.

The lack of popular involvement in the organizations has also led to a situation where the meetings of the groups are held irregularly (Inayatullah, 1972:235). In a study of the cooperative movement, Inayatullah found that most members and leaders did not expect the leadership of the organizations to be accountable to its membership (1972:234). He also found that access to information about the cooperatives was limited to the leadership and their friends. Thus the general membership of the organization was left out of the decision-making process (see Ryan, 1958:154).

The average villager did not become involved and the leadership was unable to motivate him into activity (Inayatullah, 1972:31). It should be noted that some organizations were able to motivate the villagers into self-help work but these groups are not common and seem to be confined to the Sarvodaya movement which mixes religion with self-help (Ratnapala, 1978; Ariyaratne, 1970).

The leadership of the local organizations tends to come from an elite strata at the top of village society (Wanigaratne, 1978:58; Welikala, 1972:88). Marguerite Robinson (1975:175-76) has listed the qualities that villagers in the hill country village she studied felt that leaders must possess. These include a prestigious "gedera" name;[5] high economic standing; birth in the village; being well-married; education; and a certain amount of Buddhist piety. She also lists (177-178) several criteria for success in the political arena. These are the qualities mentioned above and access to important outsiders. As she states, "leadership presupposes a command of the broker's role" (178). The study mentioned earlier by the Rural Development Training and Research Institute (Government of Sri Lanka, 1976:29) has noted that the leaders of the RDS tend to be better educated and tend to be landowners and teachers. They argue (75) that a significant qualification for leadership in the villages is the economic power of the individual selected.[6] The findings of both studies were supported by the responses of many of the MPs interviewed for this study. A UNP member of the Eighth Parliament stated that his electoral support in a village depended on the local party organization in the village.

> Everything depends on the officials of the branch. If the secretary-treasurer is influential in the village then they get the vote...My local party branches elected their own leaders. You must explain to them the type of person they must elect. You know a secretary must be influential and literate.

Robinson has also stated (1975:83) that leadership at the village level:

> is informal and non-directive, and it is leadership based upon qualities of wealth, land, and personal character. It is leadership, but is leadership through influence rather than through office...[Their] status is not derived from their office. They are leaders not because they hold office but because of who they are. Their supporters are not a solid group of followers who follow after them under any conditions, they are a fluctuating group which changes from one organization and issue to another.

Thus even though elections for these organizations are open and fair, pressure is exerted on the voters by influential leaders such as the MP, and by traditional beliefs about leadership to elect a certain strata of society to the positions of leadership.

Another factor concentrating the leadership of local groups among a few individuals is the practice of the leaders of a community to seek leadership in several organizations. As one MP stated, "if you speak to the leaders of one group, you have spoken to the leaders of all groups in the village." The same alliances of individuals struggle among themselves for the right to lead the groups.

Thus, the evidence indicates that local organizations do not have wide popular input and are dominated by an economic and social elite in the community. Added to this is the partisan nature of the organizations. This is to be expected among the local political party branches but considering that the leaders of the other organizations are chosen by democratic elections, one would expect them to reflect a wide spectrum of political thought. Not all local organizations are partisan in nature but the evidence indicates that many are. Several incidents have been cited where the RDS leadership belonged to the party opposing the government MP in the electorae. As a result, the MP formed a new RDS which was recognized by the government and the old RDS fell into disuse (see Wanigaratne, 1977:29).

THE PRESSURES PLACED ON THE MP

The analysis that follows examines how the MPs respond to certain elements in their electorates, identifying those elements and attempting to explain why they respond to them. Several types of reponsiveness can be identified; the first of these is based on long-standing ties to caste, family and region.

Before discussing the factors that influence the MPs' decisions about the placement and selection of projects, it should be noted that Sri Lankan electorates are very homogenous, especially when one considers the lack of ethnic homogeneity at the national level. The major ethnic groups, the Tamils and Sinhalese are geographically concentrated as are the Moors, although to a lesser extent. The language groups, which correspond closely to the ethnic groups are extremely concentrated with the Tamil speakers largely isolated in the north and east although there are pockets of Tamil speakers in the hill country among the Indian Tamils and in Colombo. The Sinhala speakers predominate in the other areas of the island. Caste groups are also geographically concentrated with the Goyigama, generally making up 80 to 90 percent of the population in the electorates where they are dominant while the Karawa, Salagama, Durawa, Batgam, and Wahumpara comprise a majority in most of the electorates where they are concentrated.

Most of the rural electorates are economically undiversified as well. The workforce in these electorates is primarily engaged in fishing or farming with income levels very low and very little income difference between the majority of the population. Large differences do exist between the very rich and the average citizen, but the rich are small in numbers and tend to live in the cities.

Most MPs are influenced by appeals from what might be loosely described as kinsmen. It appears that some MPs favor certain sections of their electorates, with which they are closely linked, with more DCB funds than other sections. Since most of the electorates of the island are relatively small, it is difficult to make distinctions between the various regions of an electorate. However, two electorates where geographic divisions are extremely sharp were chosen and examined. The results indicated that in both cases the MP favored his home area by providing it with more funds.

In the first electorate, the MP came from a very distinct geographic section of the electorate and represented the electorate in both parliaments. In 1976, the population of the two geographic sections of his electorate was almost the same with 26,915 in his home area and 26,898 in the section with which he was not closely associated. His home area received allocations equalling 713 thousand rupees while the other section of the electorate received just over 379 thousand rupees. Thus, the per capita allocations received by his home area were 88 percent higher than the other section of his electorate (see Table 7.7).

In 1977, an election year, he faced a stiff challenge from an ex-MP of the electorate. He easily won but charges that he favored his home area were made by the ex-MP who came from the other section of the electorate. Not surprisingly in 1977, the election year, the differences between the two sections of the electorate disappeared. The section of the electorate he is not tied to received a per capita average of about 4 percent more funds than did his home area.

In 1979, the election was behind him and the pattern of 1976 reappeared. He made almost twice as many per capita allocations to his home area as he did to the other section of the electorate.

The second example involves an MP who was first elected in 1970 and defeated in 1977. In the analysis of the DCB allocations in 1976, the region of the

TABLE 7.7
Per capita allocations of first MP

	1976	1977	1979
Region associated with MP	26.5	26.2	37.6
Other region	14.1	27.2	19.2

TABLE 7.8
Per capita allocations of second MP

	1976	1977	1979
Home area of 1970-77 MP	12.5	31.6	12.3
Other area	15.5	11.2	17.5
Unknown	4.4	4.9	6.6

electorate which he comes from received a smaller allocation of resources than did the other area (see Table 7.8). In the election year of 1977, the pattern changed and his region of the electorate received almost three times the per capita allocation of the other region of the electorate. In the election of 1977, he was the loser and his opponent, the new MP, was from the other region of the electorate. In 1979, the analysis of the new allocations revealed that the new MP allocated about 40 percent higher per capita allocations to his region of the electorate than he did to the other section of the electorate.

Thus a very distinct pattern exists in the two electorates favoring the section of the electorate that is associated with the MP of the electorate. The basis of this bias may be the desire to help the home area of the electorate of the MP or perhaps a greater familiarity of the area that leads the member to allocate more funds to it.

A second factor that may play a part in the tendency for the MP to support that section of the electorate that he comes from is that the area may contain many of his kinsmen. In three electorates where MPs were interviewed, caste distinctions played a very important part in the 1977 election campaigns of the candidates. In two of these electorates the population was roughly evenly divided between the Goyigama caste and one of the lower caste groups. In the other electorate, low caste members comprised about one-third of the population. In all three electorates charges were made that the low caste member who represented the electorate (two in the Seventh Parliament and one in the Eighth Parliament) was biased in his allocations of DCB funds. It is not easy to study the allocations within the electorates but the comments of one of the MPs involved speak for themselves. The stated goal of the MP was "to take up the liberation of my people." His people, were the members of his caste group. When asked how he allocated his DCB funds, he stated:

As far as I'm concerned, I tried to be fair to

> areas with communities that have been neglected. When communal politics comes in there is controversy. Electricity and roads stopped where the houses of the minority community began. The problem is that those who enjoyed the benefits earlier now cause trouble.

He feels that certain people in his electorate have been neglected and sees their needs as his first concern. Of course, he may have recognized the neglect of these people because he is one of them.

Another factor that leads to a caste bias in the electorates can be found in the other two electorates. These electorates are split evenly between the Goyigama, and the Wahumpara community in one and the Batgam community in the other. The MPs in the Seventh Parliament were members of the two low caste groups and were defeated by Goyigama candidates in the elections to the Eighth Parliament. The main source of support for the two candidates in each electorate was from their own caste community although each was able to gather votes from members of the other caste. This was especially the case in the 1977 elections when it appeared that large numbers of low caste voters deserted their kinsman and voted for the Goyigama candidate. Yet the main source of support for each of the four candidates according to them (all were interviewed) was from members of their own caste community.

If the supporters of a candidate are largely members of his caste community then under the prevailing system of patronage in Sri Lanka, it would be expected that the member would allocate more funds for his community than he would allocate to those who do not support him and just happen to be from another community. Patronage politics are an important part of the Sri Lankan political system. The supporters of a candidate reap the benefits of the jobs that the member has available, and in the case of development projects, the villages that support him or her receive the largest segment of the DCB allocations. Thus, patronage politics takes on the guise of communal politics and the allegations against these members are made. What appears to be actions motivated by these long standing ties to community, caste and family may have become nothing more than partisan politics as past caste biases have become enshrined in party allegiences.

In many parts of the island, whole villages line up in support for either one or the other candidate. Under these conditions it becomes very easy for MPs to perceive which areas give them support and which do not. Many of the MPs interviewed indicated that there were villages in other electorates or during the terms of other MPs in their electorates which were totally ignored because the village was believed to be full of opponents of the MP (see Ratnapala, 1978:198).[7] It is common knowledge in Sri Lanka that government benefits are given to those who support the government party. In the municipal and urban council elections of 1979, the prime minister made statements shortly before the election urging people to vote for those parties which would be able to work with the national government because otherwise the municipality might not receive development funds. Of course, his party--the UNP--was the only one which could work with the national government.[8]

The role of partisanship can be seen in the very high degree of consultation by the MPs with the local party branches on matters of development projects. The local parties are the advisors of the MPs and it is very unlikely that they will advise the MP to provide funds for communities where the opposition party dominates.

Many members made spirited defenses of their giving government benefits to their supporters. This is an accepted way of political life in Sri Lanka and apparently plays a major part in the allocation of decentralized budget funds. Yet a responsiveness to local needs on the part of the MP does not indicate that the local villagers are getting what they want but only what the MP thinks they want. Since this study focused on the MPs and their perceptions, it is not possible to make any kind of judgment on whether the MP's responsiveness was what the local population wanted. The argument presented here is that the MPs did make some effort to accommodate local interests on the basis of patronage.

THE ADMINISTRATION OF DCB PROJECTS

A very large part of the Sri Lankan national budget is left unspent. It has been estimated that 25 to 30 percent of the budget is not spent (Weerasooria, 1979, n.p.). This carries over into the DCB where administrative and technical problems lead to delays in the projects and many MPs are unable to spend their allocations by the end of the fiscal year. An attempt was made to analyze the success that the MPs had in completing their projects under the budget. Haphazard accounting procedures make this analysis questionable and its findings unconvincing.

Several problems emerged. The first was that many MPs cancelled projects if it appeared that the project would not be completed before the end of the fiscal year. This meant that only projects that were completed appeared on the fourth quarter reports of the DCB. However, the accounting procedures between districts varied and in some districts these projects were carried on the fourth quarter report while in others they were dropped. An example of the magnitude of the dropping and adding of projects can be seen in 1977 after the UNP took power in July. In Galle district, in the south of the island, close to 50 percent of the original allocations for projects were dropped from the DCB in several electorates.

A second problem in the analysis came from the type of project funded. Certain departments were better able to complete projects than were others. The Ceylon Electricity Board and the Sri Lanka Transport Board among others did not have to spend their allocations by the end of the fiscal year and therefore all of the funds they received, appeared on the fourth quarter reports as having been spent. Other departments such as the Department of Local Government or Rural Development deal with small projects that are much easier to complete and therefore usually spend the total allocation. Therefore, if members wanted to appear as if they were spending all of their allocations, they could do so by allocating the money to departments that would spend it all. The case of a minister in the Southern Province was frequently cited as an example of this. A very large proportion of his budget was allocated to rural electrification projects and thus he had the appearance of spending most of his money.

Ministers also had the advantage of pressuring the bureaucracy to act on their projects. In the case of one junior minister in Uva Province, about one to two percent of his allocation was spent by the end of the third quarter, ranking him last in the expenditure of his allocations in his district. In the fourth quarter, however, he spent almost 95 percent of his allocation and finished the year with the highest percent of allocations spent in his district.

Two opposition MPs from multi-member electorates complained that the ministers who also represented the electorates they represented received first priority when it came to the availability of materials and manpower. If anything was left over, then they would receive it. In both cases, the ministers involved were very important in the government and the SLFP MPs seemed to accept the fact that this was to be expected. Important government ministers deserve the first of everything.

The analysis of the success of spending allocations among the MPs indicated that no pattern appeared to exist between the levels of formal authority in the parliament (see Table 7.9). This may have resulted from the lack of comparability between districts which could not be controlled for because of the unavailability of data on expenditures. However, what is the most surprising finding is the relative success of the Sinhalese opposition members in spending their allocations. In two of the three years where data was available for the Sinhalese opposition parties, they had the highest success in spending their allocations. However, the

TABLE 7.9
Average percent of DCB allocations spent by MPs

	Percent Spent	Number of Cases
Backbenchers	73.3	36
Deputy ministers	71.9	10
Ministers	70.7	9
Political authorities/ district ministers	70.6	4
Sinhalese opposition parties	76.4	8
TULF	60.5	13

members of the Tamil parties, for whom data was not available before 1978, finished very low in the expenditure of their allocations. Again, this may be due to the lack of data for the Tamil areas. In any case, the data indicate that no apparent pattern exists in the expenditures and that this may be due to the unreliability of the data.

However, the success of the MPs in spending their allocations may not be an accurate measure of how well they are doing their job. Another indication of success, which is a little indirect but nevertheless indicates the significance of the linkage between the MPs and the populace and the role of the DCB in this linkage, is the general interest that the local villagers take in the projects. Several MPs stated that since the start of the DCB, local villagers have taken a greater role and interest in the projects in their electorates (see Gajanayake, n.d.:46). The interest appears to take two forms.

The first form is that of the villagers overseeing projects taking place in their electorates. Several MPs stated that the voters in their electorates came to them reporting on irregularities in the projects. Another stated in parliament that:

> When a villager sees the notice and realizes that such and such an amount has been allotted for this particular village, he would take a personal interest to see that those schemes are implemented and that the monies allotted are properly spent (Hansard, vol. 12, col. 1493).

An Assistant Director of Planning in one of the district kachcheris stated that he had observed cases where the people not only went out to check on the officials' work, but questioned them about the mixing of cement and other things (Divakala, 1979).

A second type of involvement is of more significance. This is the donation of labor and active involvement of the villagers in the projects. In the case of many small projects left to local organizations for administration, the villages are able to get volunteer workers to carry out the project and save the allocation which was either sent back to the national treasury or given to the organization for other work. This type of volunteer work is based on the traditional belief that a citizen should donate labor to the state.

Thus, evidence exists that the MPs do respond to local pressure and that the local villagers become involved, in some way, in the DCB. The involvement of the local people in the projects may be limited but it has increased since the creation of the DCB. The measurement of how successful the MPs were in actually aiding their electorates was not possible with the data available to this study and therefore was not attempted.

This chapter has argued that the MPs involve themselves very heavily in development work and that they are responsive, in some way, to their constituents. This responsiveness appears to be based on patronage. The involvement of local organizations in the planning of projects, although limited by MP control over the system and elite control over the organizations, is an important advance in providing the local population with some input into the development work in their electorate. Thus the MP acts as a link between the village, and the national government and administration in Colombo.

The last three chapters have looked at representataion in the three main components of a Sri Lankan MP's job in isolation. The final two chapters address the broader question of representation, in view of the findings of the last three chapters.

NOTES

1. Both the head of the council and the council were called the political authority. To avoid confusion, the council will be referred to as the district political authority or DPA while the head of the council will be referred to as the political authority.

2. One LSSP MP stated that his party opposed the decentralized budget because they feared that it was an SLFP attempt to take some of the power away from the minister of finance who was a member of the LSSP. The LSSP's fear of the SLFP's intentions may have been exacerbated by the fact that one of the leading proponents of the DCB was Felix Bandaranaike, an SLFP minister who was not trusted by many of the Marxists and considered to be highly partisan.

3. The Jaffna Tamils are better educated and more westernized than the Tamils along the east coast. The leadership of the Tamil

parties has generally come from the Jaffna peninsula and some Batticaloa Tamils feel that the Jaffna Tamils dominate the east coast Tamils, treating them as second class Tamils.

4. This has been the case with trade unions as well in recent years with government sponsored unions gaining members and opposition sponsored unions losing membership.

5. A "gedera" name is a type of surname associated with one's ancestral home. It is not usually used by the holder of the name except for formal purposes of identification.

6. Ryan (1958:154-55) found in the village he studied that almost all of the leaders were landowners who did not cultivate the land they owned but rather rented it to tenant farmers.

7. In some cases opponents are not ignored. A case reported in a government study (Government of Sri Lanka, 1978a:24) indicated that a public latrine had been constructed in one village. It noted that the latrine was located opposite the house of a political opponent of the MP involved in the construction of the latrine.

8. Woodward (1969:94) relates an incident from the 1952 parliamentary election campaign in which many of the UNP's candidates were reputed to have informed their constituents that "unless UNP candidates were returned in their areas the government would do nothing for their constituencies." He also notes that one MP's election was voided because of such a threat (p. 59).

8
Summary

The last five chapters have described the legislator-constituent relationship in Sri Lanka. This chapter attempts to pull the themes of those five chapters together and offer some suggestions about the nature of representation in Sri Lanka. It elaborates on four significant findings of this study. The first of these is that there are two dimensions to representation in Sri Lanka and that these dimensions tend to correspond to different components of the legislator's job. One dimension is what will be called a "standing for" dimension, which tends to correspond to the law-making component of the job, while the second dimension will be called the "acting for" dimension and corresponds to the constituency service and development work components of a Sri Lankan MP's job. These are discussed in more depth later in this chapter. When legislators "stand for" their constituents there is a tendency for the issues that they deal with to be of national importance and thus this dimension corresponds roughly to the congruence model of representation discussed in Chapter 1. When legislators "act for" their constituents on constituency service and development work, they establish a relationship that will be described as an on-going process with the legislator processing constituent demands. This dimension differs quite radically from the other and from the literature on representation in the United States. The second and third findings concern the significance of the MPs' stress on constituency service and development work. The second finding deals with the importance of this stress as a part of Third World policy needs while the third finding concerns the importance of this stress on constituency needs on Sri Lanka's relatively successful experiment with democracy. The fourth finding deals with the influence that the electoral system may exert on representation. Before discussing these four findings, several important points from the last five chapters are summarized in order to provide a background for the arguments made later in this chapter.

In Chapter 1 it is argued that representational behavior can occur in all components of a legislator's job. Representational behavior is defined as an interactive relationship between the legislators and their constituents. It was clearly shown that the Sri Lankan legislators and their constituents interacted on matters of constituency service and development work. However, there appears to be little interaction in the law-making component of their job. Chapter 4 reports that Sri Lankan constituents make very few demands for national legislation or policy on an MP. In addition, in Chapter 6 it is found that most legislators have limited power to influence law-making. This difference between the law-making, and the constituency service, and development work components of the job are discussed in more detail, later in this chapter.

In a second point in Chapter 1 it is argued that the representational role types first proposed by Eulau and associates (1959) are not applicable to the Sri Lankan legislator. This becomes quite obvious when one considers that: (1) Eulau's categories were oriented to legislator's roll call choices; and (2) that in Sri Lanka, an MP's political party dictates how the MP will vote on roll call votes. Since the Sri Lankan MPs do not have any choice about their roll call votes, Eulau's role orientations do not apply.

However, it was found that the distribution of authority in the parliament is an important factor influencing the behavior and attitudes of the Sri Lankan legislators. In a sense, the formal distribution of authority in parliament leads to different types of legislative roles with each role determined by the MP's formal authority. Yet it does not necessarily follow that the formal authority in the parliament determines how well a legislator represents his or her constituents. There is no doubt that the ministers have more resources available to assist their constituents but because of the demands of their ministry work, the ministers are unable or unwilling to give as much attention to their constituents' needs as are the backbenchers and deputy ministers.

It is argued in a third point that Sri Lankan legislators are engaged in an interactive relationship with their constituents. This relationship is marked by several features. The first of these is that constituents make demands on their legislators. This was clearly shown in matters dealing with constituency service and development work. Secondly, legislators respond to these demands. This was documented in the chapters dealing with the members' meetings with their constituents and their work with development projects. Thirdly, the legislators desire to satisfy all of their constituents' demands and are limited only by the availability of resources. The fourth factor deals with the nature of the decisions that the MPs make in the constituency service and development work components of their jobs. These decisions are of a different nature than roll call decisions. Both the third and fourth factors will be discussed in more depth later.

Having presented these observations, a discussion of the nature of representation in Sri Lanka can now be made. What emerges from the findings of this study is a perception of representation that differs quite sharply from earlier attempts to conceptualize it. As noted above, representational behavior occurred in constituency service and development work but did not appear to occur in the law-making component of the legislator's job. In constituency service and development work, the nature of the relationship between the legislator and his constituents is an interactive exchange. They have an on-going relationship, with the legislator as a processor of demands rather than a mediator. A more thorough discussion of this occurs later but for now the question to be answered is why does the law-making component of the legislator's job appear to be devoid of a representational relationship.

It would appear that the law-making component of a legislator's job is different from the other components in the way constituents are represented. As noted earlier in this chapter, there is no indication in the findings of Chapters 4 and 6 that the constituents made many demands concerning national issues and legislation. This is surprising when one considers that the Sri Lankan MPs believed that their election win or loss was the result of their national party's image and policies (see Chapter 4).

In a parliamentary system with strict party loyalty on roll call votes, most legislators do not have extensive policy making input. Thus, it should not be surprising that constituents do not make many demands concerning national issues and policies. If their legislator is not directly responsible for the policies of the national government, how do they apply pressure on the national government to obtain the policies they want? This can be done by voting against the candidate of the governing party in their electorate. Thus the voters' evaluations of the sitting MP can be based on factors that are beyond the control of the MP.

Hannah Pitkin (1967:209) has defined representation as "acting in the interest of the represented, in a manner responsive to them." She argues that the representative may act in his or her constituents' interest in two different ways. They may "stand for" their constituents or they may "act for" them. "Standing for" one's constituents involves the election of a legislature which more or less reflects the various divisions in the political system. A legislator represents not by what he or she does but by what he or she is (Pitkin, 1961:61). "Acting for" one's constituents involves "the obligations of the representative as agent" of others (Pitkin, 1967:115). Here, what the representative does is of significance and not necessarily what he or she is. These two dimensions of representation are not mutually exclusive but rather are different parts of the representational relationship.

In the law-making component of the job, the Sri Lankan MP's "stand for" their constituents. The voter makes a collective evaluation of the program and policies enacted by the governing party or offered by the opposition parties. A party is given a term of office to present its program of policies. When that term of office is up or the legislature votes no confidence in the government, the constituents then evaluate the party by re-electing or defeating it. Thus, when a voter makes a decision on how to vote, he or she takes into consideration the collective policies of the governing or challenging party in an election. In this aspect of the voters' evaluation, the candidates make no difference. The only important factor about them is their party affiliation.

Legislators also "act for" their constituents. In this dimension of representation the legislators have a personal relationship with their constituents. Here, the voter evaluates the incumbent MP on the basis of his or her individual actions.

The constituents' evaluation of the individual MP is similar to what many researchers in the United States sought to find among United States representatives. They sought to find a linkage based on the policy options taken by the legislators. In Sri Lanka, the criteria of evaluation are based on the particularized and local benefits that members can give their constituents. In this case, the legislators' individual actions are evaluated by their constituents.

Thus, constituents can make two different sets of evaluations of their legislators and parliament.[1] One set is an evaluation of the individual actions of their representative in parliament. Sri Lankan legislators believe that the collective evaluation is the deciding factor in elections. This may reflect the very serious state of the economy in Sri Lanka. The very high levels of youth unemployment coupled with the seemingly endless tradeoff between high inflation and severe restraints on the availability of consumer goods may make the national policies of the government the most important factor in voter evaluations of the candidates for parliament.

Yet in stating that national issues were the dominant factor in parliamentary elections, most MPs noted that the large majority of voters were consistent in how they voted from one election to another. Shifts in electoral fortunes were considered to be the result of "floating" voters who were a small percentage of the total voters but large enough to decide an election.

If this is the case, it would indicate that most voters remain loyal to one of the candidates or parties despite the failure of the parties to solve the problems of unemployment and inflation. This may indicate that these voters are evaluating the candidates on the basis of the particularized benefits and development work they can provide for their constituencies.[2]

It should be noted that the Sri Lankan legislator's preoccupation with particularized benefits and development work is not that unusual an activity for a Third World legislator. It does not indicate that they or their constituents are unsophisticated concerning national issues and therefore remain aloof from them because they do not understand them, nor does it indicate that the legislature has "declined" or failed in its responsibility to approach national issues. The issues of most importance to the average Sri Lankan villager may well be these questions of local development and not the overriding issues of national policy, except at a generalized level of whether the government provides certain basic services to the people. The MPs' development activities may be the most important function of the average MP in the opinion of both the legislators and their constituents. It provides the opportunity for the constituents to have some power over what the government does in the areas that most directly affect their lives.

The creation of an economic infrastructure in the rural areas of the country is perhaps the most important concern of the Sri Lankan government, and probably for any government in a developing nation. Because of this, national legislation may not be as important as it is in the United States where the maintenance of a high standard of living and the provision of economic amenities are the main objectives of the government. In western industrialized societies, government policy is meant to continue the success of the economic system. It has a national orientation affecting broad segments of the society. In a Third World society the needs are different. Their governments have been preoccupied with development (Musolf and Springer, 1979:292). In order to understand legislatures, it should be realized that the promotion of development must also be a major concern of the legislatures in these societies. Because of the localized nature of society in the Third World and the small scale of economic units, policies with national impacts may not affect the lives of villagers as much as the MPs' planning and administering of development projects in their electorates. The preoccupation with development projects in Sri Lanka and the lack of concern with national policy matters by the MPs may be a response to the needs and requirements of the nation.

A broader understanding of policy in Third World countries should include this type of rural development work done by the legislators. Issues of national importance and impact, decided in the capital city often have little direct effect on the rural areas. For example, fiscal, monetary, and foreign policies in a Third World nation do not directly affect many people because they are outside the tax structure affected by fiscal and monetary policies and have little concern with foreign affairs. The effect of the national government is most thoroughly felt in the small matters that affect the Sri Lankan villagers directly, such as jobs for their children or more water for irrigation. Beyond these and the myriad of small licensing taxes that are paid by the villagers there is little contact with the policies of the national government.

Therefore, the finding that Sri Lankan legislators are preoccupied with development work and the satisfaction of the personal needs of their constituents may not be an indication of a legislative system that has declined from its role as a maker of national policy or has been taken over by traditional loyalties, thus serving the needs of a traditional and backward peasantry, but rather may suggest a dynamic institution that has changed and adapted itself from its alien beginnings in Great Britain to fit the needs and requirements of a developing nation. Rapidly modernizing societies have different needs than do highly industrialized societies. Thus, the flexibility of the Sri Lankan parliament to adjust to the needs of the society may be an indication of the institutionalization of the legislature and its contribution to Sri Lankan development.

The types of projects undertaken by the MPs under the decentralized budget have a much greater and direct effect on the local population than national policies. If the Sri Lankan legislature is found to be representative and responsive to the needs of the people, it is because of this function and the linkage with the national government that it provides for the average villager.

Thus, if this interaction between the legislators and their constituents is of importance to policy making, it is necessary to examine this relationship in more depth. In the concept of representation as formulated in the research focusing on law-making, a legislator makes decisions which benefit some and adversely affect others. The legislators make choices with wide ranging effects that obtain the support of some and incur the opposition of others. The type of decisions made by the Sri Lankan MPs are different. First, the effects of the decisions are relatively limited, affecting either a few individuals or a village. Second, the nature of the decisions are not such that one group or individual gains and one loses. When a decision is made, it does not provide benefits to one group and refuse them to another. It is only a positive decision supporting the claim of one individual or group. All other groups who seek similar claims do not lose the opportunity or chance to obtain what they seek. In other words there are no long term losers. An individual decision is still a win or lose affair but the losers have as much chance of winning the next day as they did the day the decision was made. Thus, a job seeker who does not get a job today may be chosen for a job the next day when more jobs become available. In most cases the MPs support the claims of all those coming to them. The only constraint on their responding to the demands is the limitation of resources. Under the earlier conceptualization of representation, the legislator must support some and oppose others, and the decisions are such that there are winners and losers.

In decisions such as these the MP generally receives the benefits of making the decision and very little of the negative effects that come from governmental decisions. Since the reason for not acting in a constituent's favor is the unavailability of resources, the MP can always ascribe the blame for not providing jobs or money for development to others (Fiorina, 1977:71). In the case of development projects, government bureaucrats can be blamed for slow work or for refusing to give approval to the feasibility studies. In the case of particularized benefits, the bureaucracy may once again be blamed but it is also possible that the MPs transfer some blame for the lack of jobs to their own cabinet and thus increase the chances that the constituents will vote against their party in the next elections. An example of this can be seen in the so-called backbenchers "revolt" of December 1978. During the budget debate a series of backbenchers took the floor of parliament and accused certain unnamed ministers of circumventing the "job bank" and illegally providing jobs in their electorates. They claimed that the young people in their electorates were very angry and if things did not change they would be unable to set foot in their electorates. It is very likely that when these angry youths came to them claiming that people were getting illegal jobs, the MPs placed the blame on their ministers as they did in the public record of the parliamentary debates.

The method used by the Sri Lankan MPs to decide who must wait and who will receive what they request is patronage. It has been noted that three types of patronage exist in Sri Lanka (Jupp, 1978:238). These are communal, partisan and family. A fourth kind based on money or bribery is ignored in this discussion because of a lack of reliable data. However, it does exist and is prevalent in Sri Lanka. To receive patronage, a constituent must be a supporter of the MP or make a claim of family or communal ties. In most cases, the MPs give first to their supporters and then, if anything is left over, to the others. In the case of jobs, they either let their party branches decide who gets them or do it personally. In a few cases, MPs stated that they made these decisions on the basis of need. To a degree this was the case with most members. Many had rules that only one member of a family could receive a job. This helped to widen the benefits bestowed by the jobs. In the case of development projects, the local party branches played a role in helping the MP decide what to do. In addition, the leaders of other organizations offering advice to the MP were supporters of the MP. Those who help the MP get the largest share of the benefits but opponents of the MP sometimes also receive help. In one electorate near Kandy, the MP had found a job for the son of the man he had defeated in the 1977 elections. This was, however, an exception to the general rule of giving to your supporters.

It is within this system of interaction between the legislators and their constituents that the "acting for" dimension of representation occurs. The legislator provides a needed link between the central government and the requests of the populace for help. The legislators, acting as representatives of the government, process their constituents' demands and decide how to distribute what the government has available to assist their constituents. This process never ends as the legislator daily attends to the personal and local needs of his or her constituents. Representation occurs when the legislators attend to the needs of their constituents. If the MP makes an attempt to respond to them, then he or she is carrying out the job of representation. If they do not respond, then the constituents are not being represented. This view takes the perspective that the constituents are in a position to dictate to the legislator what the legislator must do to be representative. If they do not dictate anything to them, then the legislators may attend to other matters. Thus, representation in these two components of the job reflects this responsiveness on the part of the legislator to the demands of the constituents.

The "acting for" and "standing for" dimensions of representation are further complicated by the impact of the institutional structure they operate in. The influence of the formal levels of authority in parliament has been discussed throughout this book. However, the influence of the nature of the electoral system has been less obvious and needs further elaboration in this chapter. The two general classes of electoral systems are the single-member electoral constituency or the

Anglo-American system, and proportional representation. The type of electoral system a nation adopts has been found to have an important influence on the political system of that country (Rae 1968; Oberst 1984). However, few scholars have noted the more pervasive influence of the electoral system on the nature of the representational relationship. The single-member district has been the avenue for the personalized representation that so many Sri Lankans expect and their legislators are so willing to give. A system of proportional representation might not have allowed such a representational relationship to develop and to flourish. In fact, it is highly likely that it would not have developed under a system of proportional representation. The reader needs only to go back over the earlier chapters of this book to examine the subtle but pervasive influence of the single-member district. Constituency service and development work depend on it. The law-making component of their jobs might be transformed by proportional representation as the legislators, with little else to do, try to exert more influence over the legislative process. The pervasive influence of the electoral system in Sri Lanka should not be ignored because of its subtle nature.

The government of the Eighth Parliament of Sri Lanka has attempted several changes in the political structure of the country. All of these raise serious questions about the forms that democratic government will take and their effect on political stability in the country. Most important of these, to the discussion here, has been the institution of a system of proportional representation. Under this system, the next parliamentary elections in Sri Lanka will do away with the single-member electoral constituency. The consequences of this change will have deep reprecussions on the stability of the Sri Lankan political system. Each electoral constituency (probably based on the administrative district) will elect anywhere from five to fifteen members of parliament. Voters will vote for a party list of candidates. No candidate will be able to improve his or her chances of being elected by offering the voters jobs or the chance to meet with the MP.[3] Under this system it would be likely that there will be no electoral reason for a member to meet individually with the constituents in his or her electorate. The government has discussed the possibility of clusters of MPs available for meetings with constituents but this system would reduce the personalized nature of the relationship and also allow constituents to go shopping for a favorable decision. This would increase the burden on the MPs. Without the link to the national government that the MPs now provide, the participation of the voters may no longer be channelled into legal and constructive pursuits and as a result, the population

may no longer be supportive of a democratic system in
Sri Lanka. The view of the Sri Lankan people may have
been summed up by one informant who stated that "I
support proportional representation and everything it
involves, but who do I go to for help now?"

The view of representation presented in this study
perhaps complicates the concept by adding several new
ideas to it. The first of these is the dual nature of
the evaluation that constituents may make of a legislator's or legislature's actions. In other words, representation occurs differently in different components of
a legislator's job. In Sri Lanka the variation exists
between the law-making component, and the constituency
service, and development work components. In addition,
the constituents evaluate their representatives on two
separate and distinct planes. One plane is the "acting
for" dimension of representation such as constituency
service or development work. The second plane is the
"standing for" dimension which involves the success of
the legislator's party with national legislation. The
second addition is an idea that has begun to appear in
the literature on legislative behavior in the United
States (Fenno, 1978; Fiorina, 1977). This is the idea
of representation as a process rather than a mediation.
In this conceptualization of representation, the legislator's most important function becomes the linkage he
or she provides between the national government and the
average constituent. By linking constituents with their
rulers, he or she represents them.

This study is only a beginning to a better understanding of representation. Further research is needed
in other political systems to test whether the dual
nature of representation that is found in Sri Lanka
exists elsewhere. The unique cultural heritage of Sri
Lanka has obviously had an effect on the development of
representative political institutions in the country.
This heritage and the structure of a parliamentary
system have undoubtedly affected the development of
legislator-constituent linkages in Sri Lanka. Yet, the
evidence of research in other political systems would
indicate that this dual nature of constituent evaluations found in Sri Lanka might be found elsewhere.[4] In
addition, the interactive relationship between constituents and representatives is in need of more rigorous
conceptualization. The attitudes of the constituents
need to be surveyed to provide a better understanding of
what they want out of this relationship and what they
feel is important about the actions of the legislators.

NOTES

1. This appears to be the case in the United States as well,

although no research has directly examined it. Evidence has been found that United States constituents judge their legislators on both the constituency services they provide (Fiorina, 1977), and on a more general and collective level related to the economic well being of the nation (Kramer, 1971; Bloom and Price, 1975).

2. In the United States, the decline of competitive congressional constituencies has been attributed to the rise in importance of representatives helping their constituents circumvent bureaucratic red tape (Fiorina, 1977).

3. The government appears to be considering a change which would allow the voters to vote for both the party list and an individual on the list. The rank order on the party list would be determined by the number of votes each person on the list received.

4. See footnote 1, concerning evidence in the United States.

9
Is Parliament of Value?

The first eight chapters have presented the data and conclusions from a case study of a Third World legislature. This chapter examines some of the implications of those findings and applies them to the broader body of knowledge of Third World legislatures and development.

The overwhelming characteristic of the Sri Lankan legislature and its legislators is their preoccupation with constituency service and development work. They play a very limited role in policy making. As has been noted in chapter 1, much of the research on legislatures has stressed the policy making component of the job. Even works specifically on the Third World have focused very heavily on the policy component of the legislator's job (Verner 1981). In Sri Lanka, as in many other Third World countries, policy making is not the most important component of the legislators' jobs. If the job of many Third World "law-makers" is not to make laws, then what purposes do legislatures serve in developing nations? This chapter attempts to answer this question.

It has been a common criticism of Third World legislatures that they are merely rubber stamps for the executive branch of government. The cabinet carries out law-making and is generally dominated by the prime minister. The legislature could be eliminated and its absence could go unnoticed. In the Sri Lankan case, this situation would be an oversimplification of the Parliament's importance. The significance of the Sri Lankan Parliament does not lie in the number of policies it makes. Its value lies with several other functions it serves in the political system.

Michael Mezey (1983) in a description of the function of Third World legislatures ony briefly touches on what appears to be the most important function served by the Sri Lankan legislature. This function will, for want of a better term, be described as linkage. A combination of what many earlier writers have described as representation and/or integration. It involves the role of the parliamentarians in linking the various elites in the society to the national government. The elites linked to the government include rural as well as urban elites, and ethnic minority group elites. The linkage process includes the representation of the needs of the people, the integrative function of bringing various ethnic groups into the mainsteam of politics, and the represention of rural interests at the urban oriented national level. The remainder of this chapter describes this linkage function.

The Sri Lankan case study indicates that parliament plays a much different role than earlier writers have indicated. It is not a law-maker or a rule-setter. It does not deal with representation in the traditional sense of the concept. Instead, parliament and its members act as a linkage mechinism, moderating and filtering the demands of the rural levels to the national level of government. If one is to answer the question raised in the title of this chapter, the answer is a resounding yes! Parliament is of value and its value is indispensable to Sri Lankan society. The linkage factor occurs in several areas. These are: (1) the promotion of political stability through the representation of basic demands; (2) the mediation between urban and rural elites; and (3) the mediation between minority ethnic groups and the national government.

POLITICAL STABILITY

At the beginning of this study, it was noted that Sri Lanka, until recently, had established a very impressive record of representative and democratic government despite low levels of economic development and the relatively traditional orientations of the citizenry. One motivation for this study was to answer the question of why stable democratic and representative government succeeded for over 30 years in Sri Lanka while under similar circumstances in other countries it has failed.

It has been argued that a rapid growth in political participation before a nation has an opportunity to create stable political institutions capable of mediating the demands of the population will result in political instability (Huntington, 1968: 53-56; 1971:314-315). Samuel Huntington in his original discussion of this theory applied it to Sri Lanka (1968: 448-452). His discussion centered on the "tensions" introduced into the political system by the entry of the rural masses. There can be no question that a rapid expansion of participation occurred in Sri Lanka. It did not come with universal suffrage in 1931. The

granting of universal sufferage merely provided the
legal framework for participation. The entry of the
rural masses awaited the mobilization of the peasantry
during S.W.R.D. Bandaranaike's successful challenge to
the UNP in 1956. He recognized the power they held and
mobilized the rural peasantry to his political advantage. Thus, the rapid growth of participation began in
the mid-1950s. The increased voter participation which
reached a high point of 86.7 percent of the total
electorate in the parliamentary elections of 1977, and
the increased numbers of constituents coming to see
their legislators are indications of this increased
political involvement of the masses.

It was at this point in the 1950s that the threat
to political stability would begin and the years following 1956 have seen the assassination of a Prime
Minister, one major coup attempt, four outbursts of
serious communal rioting, a massive insurrection of
Sinhalese young people, and an uprising of the country's largest ethnic minority, all in a period of less
than thirty years. And yet, parliamentary government
has persisted in Sri Lanka.

Huntington has argued that the persistence of
political stability in the United States during the
period of rapid expansion of political participation
in the nineteenth century

> lies...in the traditional political
> institutions which existed in America
> in the seventeenth and eighteenth centuries....The multiplicity of institutions furnished multiple means of access
> to political power. Those groups unable
> to influence the national government might
> be able to dominate state or local government....With rare exceptions most of the
> significant social and economic groups in
> American society in the eighteenth and
> nineteenth centuries could find some way
> of participating in government and of compounding their influence with governmental
> authority (1968:128-129).

Thus, Huntington saw the persistence of stability in
the United States in the ability of the political
institutions to provide the people with access to
power. Although the particular details of the situation are different, a similar process appears to have
occurred in Sri Lanka. The multiple points of access
to power in the United States, a federal system of
government, were not present in Sri Lanka but a unique
combination of factors led to one political office,
that of the member of parliament, assuming the role of
demand processor. A person unable to gain access to

the government because of communal or partisan considerations could seek out a government member of parliament who was of the same community or lineage, or wait until his or her political party was in power.

The traditional beliefs about power and the political institutions created by Great Britain worked together to provide an opportunity for the MP to assume the role of government representative with the responsibility of attending to all important constituent needs. Huntington has argued that the competitive party system in Sri Lanka has led to the mediation of the "fundamental changes in the scope of political participation and the distribution of political power" (1968:452). This is perhaps an oversimplification. The competitive party system provided the impetus for the MPs to respond to constituent demands and the frequent changes of government gave all an opportunity to be listened to. However, more importantly the legislator's role as ombudsman, evolving out of the traditional beliefs about authority, resulted in the unique role of the member of parliament as a mediator of public demands.

A limitation of this mediation and its impact on political stability can be found among the Sri Lankan Tamil community. This community has consistently supported its own political parties, the Federal Party, the Tamil Congress, and the Tamil United Liberation Front. This has denied the areas represented by the Tamil parties the benefits of government patronage. In addition, the majoritarian nature of the Sri Lankan political system (see Rothman 1984) and the failure of the Tamil representatives to develop effective government coalitions with the Sinhalese parties has further denied the Sri Lanka Tamils influence over government policies and access to patronage benefits. Both of these factors can be attributed to the increased violent resistance by the Sri Lanka Tamils in the north and east of the island. For the majority of the Sri Lankan population however, the institutions of government have served to represent and mediate their demands. The Tamils, unfortunately have been left out of this process. The ethnic problem is discussed in more detail later in this chapter.

RURAL-URBAN MEDIATOR

A second consequence of linkage is the role of the legislator as a mediator between national centralized decision-makers and rural leaders. This is especially the case in development administration. A common feature of Third World nations is their domination by westernized urban elites. At the time of independence, many of the former colonial nations were being dominated by a group of leaders who had emerged from the colonial political structure. These people were able to succeed during the colonial era because of their ability to speak the language of the colonial master (English, French, Dutch etc.), and their educational and cultural background which often mirrored those of the colonial bureaucracy. As a consequence many Third World nations, including Sri Lanka, were led by men and women whose native tongue was a European language, were born into Christian families or converted to Christianity, were educated in European universities and wore western clothes. Most importantly, the new elites held urban orientations.

In Sri Lanka there is a gap between the policy makers in Colombo and the farmers in the rural areas. The gap is based on language, cultural outlook and urban orientation. Although some writers have argued that there was a shift in the elites of Sri Lanka from the western to a rural orientation (Singer,1964), this does not appear to be the case (Oberst, 1985). Among the top policy makers in Colombo, an urban orientation continues to exist. The parliamentary backbenchers provide the linkage between the urban policy makers and the farmers in the rural areas.

Since the early 1970s, there has been an increased interest in decentralized development administration in Third World nations (Conyers, 1983:99). As noted in Chapter 6, Sri Lanka has sought to decentralize its development administration. Decentralization has been viewed as a way to achieve more efficient management of economic development, better mobilization of support for development policies, democratization of development decisions, creation of greater public accountability of officials and creation of greater national self-reliance (Rondinelli et al 1984:5-9).

In order to achieve the goals listed above, an important aspect of decentralization is creating linkages between the national government and the local populace while transferring decision-making authority to the rural decision-makers. Other countries' experiences with decentralization have not been completely successful (Rondinelli 1983). Much of this is the consequence of the failure of the leadership of these countries to transfer decision-making authority to the local governmental units that are responsible for decentralized administration. There appears to be a certain amount of fear or condescension on the part of the national leadership toward the local leaders. This fear may be the result of the large cultural and educational gap between the local elites and the national leaders.

The use of the member of parliament in the decentralization process (the decentralized budget) in Sri Lanka may be an important element of linkage between the national and local decision-makers. The MPs are trusted and largely controlled by the national decision-makers. Thus, it is much more likely for them to give more authoritative power to the MPs than they might to the local leaders. The MPs act as a link between the national government and local elites.

The creation of the decentralized budget was a major step towards decentralized development administration. In has been the most successful attempt at decentralization tried by the Sri Lankan government. Other attempts such as the District Development Committees appear to be failing while attempts to decentralize the administrative departments appear to have occurred in name only with few tangible results. It may be possible that its success, limited because of too much political interference by the MPs, is a consequence of the link that the MPs provide between the national and rural elites.

ETHNIC GROUP MEDIATOR

A third consequence of linkage is its integrative function. Since independence, there has been a sharp conflict between the dominant ethnic group, the Sinhalese, and the largest ethnic minority, the Tamils. Up until this point, the ethnic problem in Sri Lanka has been largely ignored in this analysis. The existence of separate political parties representing the Tamils is an indication of the gap between the two major ethnic communities in the country. The conflict has led to increasing levels of violence and bloodshed in recent years. The violence has been marked by attacks against the Tamils and guerilla action by Tamil youths. The attacks against Tamil citizens have involved a series of riots beginning in 1977, and occurring again in 1981 and 1983 in which most of the victims have been Tamils. In addition, the army and police have gone on rampages against innocent bystanders after attacks against them by the Tamil guerillas, commonly called "tigers." The government has argued that these rampages are unauthorized and has even called them mutinies (_Hansard_ June 8, 1981:96). The guerilla action by the "tigers" has involved several well organized and trained groups carrying out terrorist actions against government targets or supporters.

The Tamil leadership has made demands for an independent Tamil state (Eelam) to be carved out of Sri Lanka. These demands have been feuled by several concerns. All of these concerns have led the TULF's constituents to make certain demands on their legislators. Without evaluating the justification or validity of the concerns they are listed below.

(1) The first concern is the language issue.

As long as the British ruled Sri Lanka, an alien language--English--was imposed upon the people. As soon as the British left the island, the issue emerged as an important point of confrontation. The Official Language Act of 1956 named Sinhala as the one official language of Sri Lanka. Tamil speakers claim that government employment which now requires Sinhala proficiency has been difficult to obtain and to keep once hired. In addition, Tamils claim to have had difficulty communicating with the government because of the use of Sinhala in government documents and communications. The government responded to some of the Tamil complaints by passing the 1966 Tamil Language Regulation allowing for the use of Tamil in certain government transactions where those involved spoke Tamil and for time to be given to government employees whose native tongue was Tamil to learn Sinhala. The implementation of this resolution has come very slowly and it still has not been implemented fully. The Constitution of 1978 gave the Tamil language special status in some government dealings, but maintained the superiority of Sinhala in the society. The naming of Tamil as a "National Language" while Sinhala remains the one "Official Language" in the 1978 Constitution did not placate the Tamil leadership and followers, and the problem remains a point of confrontation.

(2) The second concern has been the education issue. Admissions to university education are very limited and highly competitive. After independence, admissions were determined on the basis of examinations in the three languages used in the country--Sinhala, Tamil and English. Those receiving the highest scores were admitted. For many years the number of students admitted from the Tamil language exams exceeded the number that would have been expected from this group on the basis of their percentage of the total population. Many Sinhalese felt that the Tamil examiners were inflating the scores so that more Tamil students would be admitted to the universities. In the 1970s, the United Front Government of Sirimavo Bandaranaike became concerned with the better performance of the Tamil students. Quotas based on the size of each ethnic community were created and university exams became an issue of dispute. The UNP sought to defuse the issue by altering the system to one based on merit as well as quotas, but this has not removed all of the resentment felt by the Tamil youths.

(3) Employment has been a third concern. The government sector is the main source of high status jobs. As Sinhala has become more important as the language of government, the Tamil speakers have become more concerned with the access of their community to government employment. There has been a severe shortage of jobs for educated young people of all ethnic

communities since the early 1960s. The lack of jobs has been blamed for the youth insurrection led by the JVP in the early 1970s (Kearney and Jiggins, 1975). This uprising was largely among Sinhalese youths and did not involve many Tamil youths. The government's language and education policy helped to create a sense of deprivation among the Tamil youths who now also had the Sinhalese and the government to blame for their failure to find jobs commensurate with their education. This issue in particular has helped to fuel the guerilla warfare that has engulfed the northern regions of the country.

(4) The Sinhalese colonization of traditional Tamil areas has been a fourth concern. In Trincomalee, Vavuniya and Batticaloa districts, recently irrigated lands have been opened for settlement. In many areas, especially in Trincomalee, the lands have been given to Sinhalese. This has had the effect of reducing the Tamil percentage of the population in these areas. The problem has been amplified by the Mahaweli Development Project which is now opening up newly irrigated lands at a rapid pace.

(5) The fifth concern has been regional autonomy or control over significant policy decisions directly affecting the Tamils. Two of the major issues raised by this concern are discussed below.

The first issue is the number and type of development projects in Tamil areas. The Tamils feel that they have not received an adequate share of the projects available. This has especially been the case with the present government's two major development initiatives, the Mahaweli hydroelectric dam and irrigation project which is largely affecting Sinhalese areas, and the Free Trade Zone which is located near Colombo in the Sinhalese heartland. Thus, the Tamils are not benefiting from the income and jobs generated by such projects.

The second issue has been the maintenance of law and order. At the present time, the majority of police and armed forces in the Tamil areas are members of the Sinhalese ethnic group. Many of the attacks of the "tiger" groups have been directed at the Sinhalese police and soldiers. On several occasions since 1977, the police have gone on rampages where they have attacked innocent bystanders after one of their members has been attacked. Their have been charges that hundreds of innocent bystanders have been killed, large numbers of women have been raped, and homes and businesses have been looted and burned during these attacks. The government has claimed to have punished those responsible for the attacks but has failed to produce enough evidence of this to satisfy the Tamil leaders.

These concerns have been the source of many

requests and demands made to the TULF MPs by their constituents. One can not underestimate the role of the members of parliament in allieviating some of the discontent generated by the conflict between the two ethnic groups. The Tamils have had relatively limited representation in the Sri Lankan cabinets formed since independence. The members of the Federal Party, the Tamil Congress, and the TULF have been the major representatives of Tamil interests in the government. They have acted as intermediaries between the Sinhalese dominated government and the Tamil citizenry in the north and east of the island. Complaints about the use of Tamil in dealings with the government, employment concerns, or complaints about the police have all been presented to the Tamil MPs. Although the power of the MPs to do anything about these complaints is relatively limited, they have tried, and on occasions have resolved the problem successfully. Even when they fail to find a solution, the petitioner has had the satisfaction of a listener who is concerned with their plight.

Because of the patronage system, the MPs lack the power to help their constituents. The evidence presented in this study indicates that patronage may be denied the Tamils because they have persisted in electing to parliament, members of parties which have never had an extremely active role in government policy making (the TULF, TC, FP). The small amount of patronage provided the Tamil MPs and the hope that more government benefits will be provided in the future, have helped to provide a certain amount of consolation to the Tamil constituents.

The activities of the Tamil members of parliament, eventhough most are from an opposition party-- the TULF, have acted to mediate the problems between the two ethnic groups. The Tamil MPs have been spokesmen of Tamil needs at the national level. They have also used their leverage to obtain some concessions from the government. Most importantly, they have provided an outlet for the discontent of Tamil youths. They were a source of advice and counsel which had national power connections. This outlet has helped to alleviate the tensions and potential for violence that have existed since the 1950s in the Tamil areas. Despite the limited amount of patronage available, there are some jobs available for the TULF members as well as benefits generated by their decentralized budget projects.

In October 1983, the government passed the sixth amendment to the constitution. It states that all members of parliament must recite a loyalty oath which disavows support for separatism. As a result of this oath, all of the members of the TULF were forced to leave parliament. Shortly after they were removed from parliament, the ethnic conflict intensified and the communal situation deteriorated. Throughout much of 1984, violence occurred on a daily basis in the Northern Province. The year 1985 began with President Jayawardene announcing that his government would no longer negotiate with the TULF until they dropped their demands for an independent state. This further isolated the former parliamentary leadership of the Tamils. The outlet that the MPs once provided for the Tamil youths no longer exists, and the credibility of the moderate path they advised has declined. The more radical guerilla organizations have challenged the former TULF MPs for the leadership of the Tamil people. The existence of the parliamentary representatives may not have prevented the increased levels of violence in the country but it did provide a force for alleviating the conditions leading to violence.

SUMMARY

In summary, the legislators of the Sri Lankan parliament serve a vital service for the political stability of the country, and in linking the nation's citizens with their representatives in Colombo. They have been a significant factor in alleviating three problems faced by most developing nations--ethnic conflict, political instability, and urban-rural cleavages. They alone can not resolve or prevent the problems as the rise of violence in the 1980s indicates. However, the linkage function can provide outlets for the dissatisfaction and discontent of the citizenry.

The adaptability and resiliency of the Sri Lankan Parliament should be a source of pride for the Sri Lankan people. The legislature has played an important role in the first 35 years of Lankan independence since the colonial era. One can only hope that the present and future leaders of the country realize the significance of providing outlets for the dissent and expression of all citizens. Representative democracy requires citizen input into the operation of government, and a government prepared to serve all citizens. The members of parliament have been the main force achieving these goals. The decline of parliamentary power under the 1978 Constitution, the growth of the patronage system, and the exclusion of the Tamils from the political process all raise serious questions about the continuation of stable government and the role of the MPs as links between the government and the people.

Appendix
Topics Covered
in Interviews

1. Contact between constituents and their MPs.
    a. How many people come to see them and the reasons why?
    b. How much mail do they receive?
    c. How often are they in their electorates?
    d. How often do they meet with their constituents?

2. What types of interest groups come to see the MPs?
    a. What types of requests do they make?
    b. How often do they come?

3. How do the MPs decide to spend your decentralized budget funds?
    a. Who is involved in the decision?
    b. What types of problems do they run into administering the projects?

4. Why did the MP become involved in politics?
    a. What did they hope to achieve in parliament?
    b. Were any members of their family involved in politics?
    c. Why did they join (or leave) their political party?

5. What do they consider to be the most important part of their job as a member of parliament?
    a. How much influence do they have in the making of laws?
    b. How effective are the consultative committees?

6. In the last election, who voted for them?
    a. Why did they vote for or against them?
    b. Was caste an important factor?

7. What changes have they seen in their electorate over their political career?

Selected Bibliography

Abayasekera, G. (1976) "Population Growth and Distribution in Sri Lanka." In Demographic Training and Research Unit of the University of Sri Lanka, <u>Population Problems of Sri Lanka</u>. Colombo: University of Sri Lanka.
Abeynaike, H.B.W. (1978) <u>Ceylon Daily News Parliament of Sri Lanka, 1977</u>. Colombo: Associated Newspapers of Ceylon, Limited.
_____, ed., (1965) <u>Ceylon Daily News Parliament of Ceylon, 1965</u>. Colombo: Associated Newspapers of Ceylon, Limited.
_____ and H.P. Ameratunga (1971) <u>Ceylon Daily News Parliament of Ceylon, 1970</u>. Colombo: Associated Newspapers of Ceylon, Limited.
Abeyesundere, A.N.A. (1976) "Recent Trends in Malaria Morbidity and Mortality in Sri Lanka." In Demographic Training and Research Unit of the University of Sri Lanka, <u>Population Problems of Sri Lanka</u>. Colombo: University of Sri Lanka.
Almond, Gabriel A. and G. Bingham Powell (1978) <u>Comparative Politics: System, Process and Policy</u>. Boston: Little Brown and Co.
Alpert, Eugene J. (1979) "A Reconceptualization of Representational Role Theory." <u>Legislative Studies Quarterly</u> IV, November.
Ariyaratne, A.T. (1970) <u>Sarvodaya Shramadana: Growth of a People's Movement</u>. Colombo: Sarvodaya Shramadana Movement.
Bailey, F.G. (1960) "Traditional Society and Representation: A Study in Orissa." <u>Archives of European Sociology</u> 1:121-141.
Bansil, P.C. (1971) <u>Ceylon Agriculture: A Perspective</u>. Delhi: Dhanpat Rai and Sons.
Barker, Anthony P. and Michael Rush (1970) <u>The Member of Parliament and His Information</u>. London: George Allen and Unwin.
Blondel, Jean (1973) <u>Comparative Legislatures</u>. Englewood Cliffs, New Jersey: Prentice-Hall.
Bloom, Howard and H. Douglas Price (1975) "Voter Response to Short-Run Economic Conditions." <u>The American Political Science Review</u> 69:1240-54.
Boynton, George Robert and Chong Lim Kim, eds. (1975) <u>Legislative Systems in Developing Countries</u>. Durham, North Carolina: Duke University Press.
Chee, Chan Heng (1976) "The Role of Parliamentary Politicians in Singapore." <u>Legislative Studies Quarterly</u> I (August):423-441.

Clausen, Aage (1973) *How Congressmen Decide: A Policy Focus*. New York: St. Martin's Press.
Collins, Sir Charles (1966) "Ceylon: The Imperial Heritage." In Ralph Braibanti ed., *Asian Bureaucratic Systems Emergent from the British Imperial Tradition*. Durham, North Carolina: Duke University Press.
Conyers, Diana (1983) "Decentralization: The Latest Fashion in Development Administration?" *Public Administration and Development* 3:97-109.
Davidson, Roger (1969) *The Role of the Congressman*. New York: Pegasus.
De Silva, Colvin R. (1953) *Ceylon Under the British Occupation 1795-1833*. Colombo: Apothecaries.
Devaraj, P. (1984) "Indian Tamils of Sri Lanka—Identity Stabilisation and Inter-ethnic Interaction." In Social Scientists Association eds. *Ethnicity and Social Change in Sri Lanka*. Colombo: Social Scientists Association.
Divakala, S. (1979) Personal Interview at Mannar Kachcheri, May, 1979.
Eldersveld, Samuel J. and Bashiruddin Ahmed (1978) *Citizens and Politics: Mass Political Behavior in India*. Chicago: University of Chicago Press.
Eulau, Heinz and Paul D. Karps (1977) "The Puzzle of Representation: Specifying Components of Responsiveness." *Legislative Studies Quarterly* II (August):233-254.
_____. (1978) "Policy Representation as an Emergent: Toward a Situational Analysis." In Heinz Eulau and John C. Wahlke eds., *The Politics of Representation: Continuities in Representation*. Beverly Hills, California: Sage.
Eulau, Heinz, John C. Wahlke, William Buchanan, and Leroy C. Ferguson (1959) "The Role of the Representative: Some Empirical Observations on the Theory of Edmund Burke." *American Political Science Review* 53:742-756.
_____. (1962) *The Legislative System: Explorations in Legislative Behavior*. New York: John Wiley.
Farmer, B.H. (1962) "*Politics in Ceylon*." In Saul Rose (ed.), Politics in Southern Asia. New York: St. Martin's Press.
Fenno, Richard F. (1978) *Home Style: House Members in Their Districts*. Boston: Little Brown.
Fernando, Neil (1973) *Regional Administration in Sri Lanka*. Colombo: Academy of Administrative Studies.
Fiorina, Morris P. (1977) *Congress: Keystone of the Washington Establishment*. New Haven: Yale University Press.
Gamage, Cyril (1978) "Regional Organisations for Planning and Plan Implementation—Some Trends in Participation in Sri Lanka." *Marga* 5:14-37.
Gajanayake, Stanley (n.d.) *Halpa Village*. Colombo: Government of Sri Lanka-Rural Development Training and Research Institute.
Goodman, Allan E. (1975) "Correlates of Legislative Constituency Service in South Vietnam. In George Boynton and Chong Lim Kim, (eds.), *Legislative Systems in Developing Countries*. Durham, North Carolina: Duke University Press.
Goodman, Paul (1967) "The First American Party System." In William N. Chambers and Walter Dean Burnham (eds.), *The*

American Party Systems: Stages of Political Development. New York: Oxford University Press.

Government of Sri Lanka (Ceylon) (1935) Report of the Commission on the Headman System. Sessional Paper XXVII. Colombo: Government of Sri Lanka.

_____, Ministry of Finance (1951) Economic and Social Development of Ceylon 1926-50. Colombo: Ministry of Finance.

_____. (1951a) "Report of the Bribery Commissioner, 1948-49." Parliamentary Series Number 1 of the First Parliament. Colombo: Government of Sri Lanka.

_____. (1960) "The Reports of the Parliamentary Bribery Commission, 1959-60." Parliamentary Series Number 1 of the Fifth Parliament. Colombo: Government of Sri Lanka.

_____, Department of Census and Statistics (1974) The Population of Sri Lanka. Colombo: Department of Census and Statistics.

_____, Academy of Administrative Services (1975) The District Political Authority System: Report of Government Agent's Workshop. Colombo: Academy of Administrative Services.

_____, Department of Rural Development (1976) The Role of Rural Development Societies in Sri Lanka. Colombo: Rural Development Training and Research Institute.

_____. (1978) The Constitution of the Democratic Socialist Republic of Sri Lanka. Colombo: Government Publications Bureau.

_____. (1978a) Second Interim Report to his Execellency the President of Sri Lanka by the Commission Appointed under Section 2 of the Commission of Inquiry Act (Chapter 393) to Inquire into Malpractices in Local Bodies (Municipalities) During the Period Specified in the Schedule of the Warrant. Sessional Paper V. Colombo: Government of Sri Lanka.

_____. Ministry of Plan Implementation (1979a) The Decentralised Budget in Sri Lanka. Colombo: Ministry of Plan Implementation.

_____. Department of Census and Statistics (1983) Statistical Abstract of the Democratic Socialist Republic of Sri Lanka 1977. Colombo: Government Publications Bureau.

Gunasekera, Alex (1978) "Rajakariya or the Duty to the King in the Kandyan Kingdom of Sri Lanka" in Wendy Doniger O'Flaherty and J. Duncan M. Derrett, The Concept of Duty in South Asia. New Delhi: Vikas Publishing.

Huntington, Samuel P. (1968) Political Order in Changing Societies. New Haven, Connecticut: Yale University Press.

_____. (1971) "The Change to Change." Comparative Politics 3:283-322.

Inayatullah (1972) Cooperatives and Development in Asia: A Study of Cooperatives in Fourteen Rural Communities of Iran, Pakistan and Ceylon. Geneva: United Nations Research Institute for Social Development.

International Labour Office (1971) Matching Employment Opportunities and Expectations: a Programme of Action for Ceylon. Geneva: International Labour Office.

Jayamaha, Gratien (1976) "The Growth of Public Expenditure in Sri Lanka, 1960-1975." Staff Studies (Central Bank of Sri Lanka) 6 (September):71-87.

Jayawardene, Junius Richard (1979) Personal interview on February 23.
Jennings, Sir W. Ivor (1948) "The Ceylon General Election of 1947." University of Ceylon Review 6 (July).
Jewell, Malcolm E. (1983) "Legislator-Constituency Relations and the Representative Process." Legislative Studies Quarterly 8:303-337.
Jewell, Malcolm E. and Gerhard Loewenberg (1979) "Editor's Introduction: Toward a New Model of Legislative Representation." Legislative Studies Quarterly IV (November):485-498.
Jha, Dayadhar (1977) State Legislature in India. New Delhi: Abhinav.
Jiggins, Janice (1979) Caste and Family in the Politics of the Sinhalese, 1947-1976. London: Cambridge University Press.
Jupp, James (1978) Sri Lanka: Third World Democracy. Colombo: K.V.G. de Silva and Sons.
Kahawita, R. (1979) "How the Scheme Should Work." Tribune January 20.
Karunatilake, H.N.S. (1975) "The Impact of Welfare Services in Sri Lanka on the Economy." Staff Studies (Central Bank of Sri Lanka) 5 (April):201-232.
Kearney, Robert N. (1967) Communalism and Language in the Politics of Ceylon. Durham, North Carolina: Duke University Press.
_____. (1971) Trade Unions and Politics in Ceylon. New Delhi: Thomson Press.
_____. (1973) The Politics of Ceylon (Sri Lanka). Ithaca, New York: Cornell University Press.
_____. (1966) "Ceylon: The Contemporary Bureaucracy." In Ralph Braibanti (ed.), Asian Bureaucratic Systems Emergent from the British Imperial Tradition. Durham, North Carolina: Duke University Press.
Kearney, Robert N. and Janice Jiggins (1975) "The Ceylon Insurrection of 1971." Journal of Commonwealth and Comparative Politics XIII:40-64.
Kim, Chong Lim, Joel D. Barkun, Ilter Turan and Malcolm E. Jewell (1983) The Politics of Representation in Kenya, Korea and Turkey. Durham, North Carolina: Duke University Press.
Knox, Robert (1956) An Historical Relation of the Island of Ceylon. Republished as Ceylon Historical Journal VI (July 1956-April 1957).
Kodikara, Shelton U. (1970) "Communalism and Political Modernisation in Ceylon." Modern Ceylon Studies I:94-114.
Kramer, Gerald (1971) "Short-term Fluctuations in U.S. Voting Behavior, 1896-1965." American Political Science Review 65:131-143.
Leitan, G.R.T. (1976) "The Role of the Government Agent in Sri Lanka." Journal of Administration Overseas XV (January):15-25.
Levy, Yael (1974) Malaysia and Ceylon: A Study, of Two Developing Centres. Beverly Hills, California: Sage.
Loewenberg, Gerhard (1972) "Comparative Legislative Research." In Samuel C. Patterson and John C. Wahlke, (eds.) Comparative Legislative Behavior: Frontiers of Research. New York: John Wiley and Sons.

_____ and Samuel C. Patterson (1979) <u>Comparing Legislatures</u>.
   Boston: Little, Brown and Co.
MacRae, Duncan (1952) "The Relation Between Roll-Call Votes and
   Constituencies in the Massachusetts House of Representatives."
   <u>American Political Science Review</u>, 46:1046-1055
_____. (1958) <u>Dimensions of Congressional Voting</u>. Berkeley: University of California Press.
Maheshwari, Shriram (1976) "Constituency Linkage of National Legislators in India." <u>Legislative Studies Quarterly</u> I
   (August):331-354.
Manor, James ed. (1984) <u>Sri Lanka in Change and Crisis</u>.
   London: Croom Helm.
Matthews, Bruce (1982) "District Development Councils in Sri
   Lanka." <u>Asian Survey</u> XXII:1117-1134.
Mead, George Herbert (1956) <u>On Social Psychology: Selected Papers</u>.
   Chicago: University of Chicago.
Mezey, Michael (1972) "The Functions of a Minimal Legislature: Role
   Perceptions of Thai Legislators." <u>Western Political Quarterly</u>
   25:686-701.
_____. (1976) "Constituency Demands and Legislative Support: An
   Experiment." <u>Legislative Studies Quarterly</u> I
   (February):101-28.
_____. (1979) <u>Comparative Legislatures</u>. Durham, North
   Carolina: Duke University Press.
_____. (1983) "The Functions of Legislatures in the World." <u>Legislative Studies Quarterly</u> 8:511-550.
Mohapatra, Manindra Kumar (1976) "The Ombudsmanic Role of Legislators in an Indian State." <u>Legislative Studies Quarterly</u> I
   (August):295-314.
Musolf, Lloyd ed. (1979) <u>Legislatures in Development</u>. Durham,
   North Carolina: Duke University Press.
Namasivyam, S. (1950) <u>The Legislatures of Ceylon</u>. London: Faber
   and Faber.
Narain, Iqbal and Shashi Lata Puri (1976) "Legislators in an Indian
   State: A Study of Role Images and the Pattern of Constituency
   Linkages." <u>Legislative Studies Quarterly</u> I (August):315-330.
Nugawela, L. and M.M. Wedderburn (1935) "Dissent of M.M. Wedderburn
   and L. Nugawela to the Report of the Commission on the Headman
   System." Sessional Paper XXVII. Colombo: Government of Sri
   Lanka (Ceylon).
Oberst, Robert (1977) "Partisan Politics and Economic Planning in
   Sri Lanka." Unpublished manuscript.
_____. (1984) "Proportional Representation and Electoral System
   Change in Sri Lanka." In James Manor ed., <u>Sri Lanka in Change
   and Crisis</u>. London: Croom Helm.
_____. (1984a) "The Politics of Change: Ideology and Structure in
   Sri Lanka." <u>Asian Thought and Society</u> IX:57-64.
_____. (1985) "Democracy and the Persistance of Westernized Elite
   Dominance in Sri Lanka." <u>Asian Survey</u> XXIV.
_____. (1985a) "Legislators and Ethnicity in a Third World
   Democracy." <u>Pacific Affairs</u> 58.
Ong, Michael (1976) "The Member of Parliament and His Constituency: The Malaysian Case." <u>Legislative Studies Quarterly</u> I
   (August):405-421.

Perera, Jayantha and Georg Krause (1977) The Role of Local Groups in Rural Development: A Case Study. Colombo: Agrarian Research and Training Institute.

Perera, N.M. (1964) "Comments of the Brains Trust." In Institute of Chartered Accountants of Ceylon (eds.) The Constitution and Public Finance in Ceylon. Colombo: Institute of Chartered Accountants of Ceylon.

Pfaffenberger, Bryan (1983) Caste in Tamil Culture: The Religious Foundations of Sudra Domination in Tamil Sri Lanka. Syracuse, New York: FACS Publications.

Phadnis, Urmila (1976) Religion and Politics in Sri Lanka. New Delhi: Manohar Book Service.

Pitkin, Hannah (1967) The Concept of Representation. Berkeley: University of California Press.

Ponnanbalam, Satchi (1983) Sri Lanka: National Conflict and the Tamil Liberation Struggle. London: Zed Books.

Puri, Shashi Lata (1978) Legislative Elite in an Indian State: A Case Study of Rajasthan. New Delhi: Abhinav.

Pye, Lucien (1966) Aspects of Political Development. Boston: Little Brown and Co.

Rae, Douglas (1967) The Political Consequences of Electoral Laws. New Haven: Yale University Press.

Ratnapala, Nandasena (1978) Community Participation in Rural Development. Colombo: Sarvodaya Research Institute.

Robinson, Marguerite S. (1975) Political Structure in a Changing Sinhalese Village. New York: Cambridge University Press.

Rondinelli, Dennis A. (1983) "Implementing Decentralization Programmes in Asia: a Comparative Analysis." Public Administration and Development 3:181-207.

Rondinelli, Dennis A., John R. Nellis and G. Shabbir Cheema (1984) Decentralization in Developing Countries: A Review of Recent Experience. Washington: The World Bank.

Rothman, Jay (1984) "Majority Rule and Ethnic Conflict in Sri Lanka." Paper presented at the first International Council Meeting for the Facilitation of International Conflict Resolution, College Park, Maryland.

Ryan, Bryce (1953) Caste in Modern Ceylon. New Brunswick, New Jersey: Rutgers University Press.

_____. (1958) Sinhalese Village. Coral Gables, Florida: University of Miami Press.

Samaraweera, Vijaya (1973) "The Development and Administrative System from 1802 to 1832." In Kingsley M. De Silva (ed.), History of Ceylon, vol. III. Colombo: University of Ceylon.

Scott, James C. (1972) "Patron-Client Politics and Political Change in Southeast Asia." In the American Political Science Review 66:91-113.

Shannon, Wayne W. (1968) Party, Constituency and Congressional Voting. Baton Rouge: Louisiana State University Press.

Simon, Herbert A. (1961) Administrative Behavior. New York: Macmillan.

Singer, Marshall R. (1964) The Emerging Elite. Cambridge, Massachusetts: Massachusetts Institute of Technology Press.

Siriwardane, C.D.S. (1966) "Buddhist Reorganization in Ceylon." In Donald E. Smith (ed.), South Asian Politics and Religion.

Princeton: Princeton University Press.
Smith, Donald E. (1966) "The Political Monks and Monastic Reform." In Donald E. Smith, (ed.), South Asian Politics and Religion. Princeton: Princeton University Press.
Sri Lanka Foundation Institute (1979) Proceedings of the Seminar on: A Practical Approach towards Solving the Unemployment Problem in Sri Lanka. Colombo: Sri Lanka Foundation Institute.
Stokes, Donald E. and Warren E. Miller (1963) "Constituency Influence in Congress." American Political Science Review 57:45-56.
Styskal, Richard A. (1975) "Some Aspects of Group Representation in the Phillipine Congress." In Boynton, George and Chong Lim Kim (eds.), Legislative Systems in Developing Countries. Durham: Duke University Press.
Subasinghe, D.W. (1977) "The State Sector in the Economy of Sri Lanka." In No Author, The Role of State Sector in Developing Countries. New Delhi: People's Publishing House.
Turner, Julius (1951) Party and Constituency: Pressures on Congress. Baltimore: Johns Hopkins Press.
Verner, Joel G. (1981) "Legislative Systems and Public Policy: A Comparative Analysis of 78 Developing Countries." The Journal Of Developing Areas. 15:275-296.
Wahlke, John C. (1975) "Introduction." In Samuel C. Patterson, Ronald D. Hedlund, and George Robert Boynton, Representatives and Represented. New York: John Wiley and Sons.
Wanigaratne, R.D. (1976) The Uhana Colony Village. Colombo: Agrarian Research and Training Institute and the Ministry of Information and Broadcasting.
_____. (1977) The Ambana Village. Colombo: Agrarian Research and Training Institute and the Ministry of Information and Broadcasting.
_____. (1978) A Study of Four Villages. Colombo: Agrarian Research and Training Institute and the Ministry of Information and Broadcasting.
Wanigesekera, Earle (1977) "Popular Participation and Local Level Planning in Sri Lanka." Marga 4:37-77.
Weerasooria, Wickreme (1978) "It's Actually Happening." Sunday Observer September 24.
Weerawardana, I.D.S. (1960) Ceylon General Election 1956. Colombo: M.D. Gunasena.
Weinbaum, Marvin G. (1975) "Classification and Change in Legislative Systems: With Particular Application to Iran, Turkey, and Afghanistan." In George R. Boynton and Chong Lim Kim (eds.), Legislative Systems in Developing Countries. Durham, North Carolina: Duke University Press.
Weiner, Myron (1962) The Politics of Scarcity: Public Pressure and Political Response in India. Chicago: University of Chicago Press.
Welikala, G.H.F. (1972) "Youth Leadership in Local Organizations." Marga I:86-97.
Wherre, K.C. (1963) Legislatures. New York: Oxford University Press.
Wickremeratne, L.A. (1973) "Education and Social Change, 1832 to

c. 1900." In K.M. De Silva (ed.), The History of Ceylon Vol. III. Colombo: University of Ceylon Press.
Wight, Martin (1946) The Development of the Legislative Council, 1606-1945. London: Faber and Faber.
Wilson, A. Jeyaratnam (1966) "The Tamil Federal Party in Ceylon Politics." Journal of Commonwealth Political Studies 4 (July):117-137.
_____. (1966) "Factors in the Working of Parliamentary Institutions in Ceylon." Young Socialist 4:13-23.
_____. (1974) Politics in Sri Lanka, 1947-73. New York: Saint Martin's Press.
_____. (1979) Politics in Sri Lanka, 1947-79. New York: Humanities Press, 1979.
_____. (1980) The Gaullist System in Asia: The Constitution of Sri Lanka (1978). London: Macmillan Press.
Wiswa Warnapala, W.A. (1974) Civil Service Administration in Ceylon: A Study in Bureaucratic Adaptation. Colombo: Department of Cultural Affairs.
Wiswa Warnapala, W.A., and L. Dias Hewagama (1983) Recent Politics in Sri Lanka: The Presidential Election and Referendum of 1982. New Delhi: Navrang.
Wood, Leonard (1961) Crime and Aggression in Changing Ceylon. Philadelphia: American Philosophical Society.
Woodward, Calvin A. (1969) The Growth of a Party System in Ceylon. Providence: Brown University Press.
Wriggins, W. Howard (1960) Ceylon: Dilemmas of a New Nation. Princeton, New Jersey: Princeton University Press.
Ziegler, Harmon and Michael Baer (1969) Lobbying: Interaction and Influence in American State Legislatures. Belmont, California: Wadsworth.

Index

Abeynaike, H.B.W., 38
Abeysundere, A.N.A., 57
Ahmed, Bashiruddin, 38
Almond, Gabriel, 38
Alpert, Eugene J., 10(n4)
Ambattar caste, 16
Appointed MPs. see Members of parliament, appointed MPs
Ariyaratne, A.T., 109

Baer, Michael, 23
Bailey, F.G., 2
Bandaranaike,
    Felix, 118(n2)
    S.W.R.D., 18, 77
    Sirimavo, 18, 77-78
Barker, Anthony P., 71(n4)
Batgam Caste, 16, 114
Blondel, Jean, 73
Bloom, Howard, 130(n)
Boynton, George Robert, 3
Brokers. See Political brokers
Buddhism, 15
Burghers, 14

Cabinet, 10(n9), 17, 74-77
    cabinet papers, 74, 76
    concentration of power, 74-77
    role of parliamentary group, 78-79
Cabinet ministers, 74-77
    bills presented to parliament, 75-76
    and consultative committees, 82-83
Caste system, 15-16, 111-112, 113-114
    and elections, 52(n13)

Caste system (cont'd)
    Sinhalese, 15-16
    Tamil, 16
Ceylon Moors. See Sri Lanka Moors
Ceylon Tamils. See Sri Lanka Tamils
Ceylon Workers Congress (CWC), 21(n), 94(n4). See also Political party system
Chee, Chan Heng, 2, 30(n5)
Christianity, 15(table)
Claussen, Aage, 4
Collins, Sir Charles, 51
Colombo, 21(n9)
Communist Party (CP), 12, 18, 19, 21(n13), 72n16, 74-75, 84, 94(n4), 101. See also Political party system
Constituent meetings, 55-65, 67-70
    Brokers, 62-64, 71(n8)
    Legislative attitudes toward, 67-70,
    mail, 60, 71(n4)
    visits, 55-65, 67-69
    Women, 63, 71(n6)
Constitutions,
    Donoughmore, 81-82
    1972, 16
    1978, 10(n7), 10(n8), 10(n10), 16, 17, 20(n), 21(n11), 21(n14), 22(n17), 94(n1), (n7), 141
    Sixth Amendment, 19, 95(n15), 141-142
    Soulbury, 16, 17, 82

Consultative Committees,
    81-84
    constituency function,
        82-84
    MPs' attitudes toward,
        82-83
Conyers, Diana, 137
Corruption, 44, 52(n3), (n15),
    66-68, 71(n13), (n14)

Daniel, Anura, 71(n13)
Davidson, Roger, 23
De Silva, Colvin R., 46, 47
Debates. See
    Parliamentary debates
Decentralized Budget (DCB),
    97-118, 137-138
    administration of, 115-118
    allocations, 99-118
    organizations involved,
        104-111
    political authority, 97-98,
        99-102, 118(n1)
    political pressure, 111-115
    pre-DCB era, 97-98
    project selection, 103-109
Devaraj, P., 14
District administration, 17,
    21(n16),
District development committees,
    138
District ministry, 30(n4). See
    also Decentralized budget
Divakala, S., 117-118
Donoughmore Constitution. See
    Constitutions
Durawa caste, 15

Educational system,
    growth, 57-58
    university admissions, 139
Eelam, 138
Eldersveld, Samuel, 38
Elections,
    description, 18-19
    finances, 67
    incumbancy and re-election,
        43-44
    and participation, 51
    presidential, 18-19
    referendum, 19
    voter choice, 43-44
Electoral system, See
    Proportional representation

Ethnic Groups, 13-15
    conflict, 20, 136, 138-142
    minorities oversampled 13,
        21(n5)
    representation in parliament,
        14(table)
Eulau, Heinz, 1, 2, 3-4, 8,
    9(n2), (n4), 122

Farmer, B.H., 53(n26)
Federal Party (FP), 19, 84, 85,
    92, 101-102, 136, 141.
    See also Tamil United
    Liberation Front
Fenno, Richard F., 2, 4, 5, 23,
    130
Fernando, Neil, 50
Fiorina, Morris P., 2, 9, 127,
    130, 130(n), 131(n2)
Free Trade Zone, 140

Gajanayake, Stanley, 109, 117
Gamage, Cyril, 98
Goodman, Allan E., 2, 52(13)
Goodman, Paul, 53(n18)
Government Agent, 17-18, 50, 51
    powers 17-18
Goyigama caste, 15, 21(n10),114
Great Britain,
    colonial rule 13, 45, 47-51
    view of Ceylon, 45, 53(n19)
Gunasekera, Alex, 46, 47

Headmen, 47, 49, 51
Hewagama, L. Dias, 22(n18)
Hinduism, 15(table)
Huntington, Samuel P., 2,
    134-136.

Inayatullah, 109
Independents, 12, 19, 84
India, 30(n5), 52(n8)
Indian Tamils, 14,21(n8)
    Denial of Citizenship 14
Interest Groups, 33-34, 35-36,
    38-42
    and administration, 39
    local, 41-44, 104-111
    national, 38-41, 43-44
    personalization of, 40-41, 43
    and political parties, 39, 40
    trade unions, 30(n3), 39-40,
        42, 52(n9), 119(n4)

155

International Labour
   Organization, 57

Jayamaha, Gratien, 56
Jayawardene,
   Junius Richard, 18-19, 78,
      82, 108, 142
   M.D.H., 30(n6), 94(n12)
Jewell, Malcolm E., 4, 23
Jha, Dayadhar, 52(n8)
Jiggins, Janice, 15, 21(n10),
   40, 140
Job bank, 65-67
Job seekers. See Members of
   parliament, employment; and
   Unemployment
Jupp, James, 40, 41, 53(n26),
   127

Kachcheri system, 50-51,
   53(n25), (n26). See also
   Local government
Kahawita, R., 50
Karawa caste, 15
Karayar caste, 16
Karps, Paul, 2, 3, 4, 8, 9(n4),
Karunatilake, H.N.S., 56, 71(n2)
Kearney, Robert N., 30(n3), 38,
   39, 40, 49, 78, 81, 82, 140
Kim, Chong Lim, 3
Knox, Robert, 46, 47
Kodikara, Shelton U., 48
Kotelawala, John, 77-78
Koviyar caste, 16
Kramer, Gerald, 130(n)
Krause, Georg, 64

Lanka Sama Samaja Party (LSSP),
   12, 18, 19, 42, 74-75, 84,
   94(n4), 101, 118(n2)
Law-making, 25-29
Leitan, G.R.T., 50
Levy, Yael, 46
Local government, 48-50
   colonial era, 48-50, 53(n23),
      (n25)
   pre-colonial, 53(n22)
Loewenberg, Gerhard, 1, 2, 3, 23

MacRae, Duncan, 3, 5
Mahaweli project, 140
Maheshwari, Shriram, 2
Mail. See Members of
   parliament, mail received

Malays, 14
Matthews, Bruce, 17
Mead, George Herbert, 5-6
Members of Parliament,
   appointed, 17, 19, 92-93
   attitudes toward job, 26-29,
      67-70
   employment function, 36-37,
      44-45, 57-58
   formal authority and job,
      24-30
   importance of job, 26-30
   mail received, 60, 71(n4)
   meetings with constituents,
      34-37, 55-65, 67-69
   motivation, 45
   parliamentary group meetings,
      77-81
   private members' bills, 88-89
   question time, 85-88
   rebel members, 26-29, 34-35,
      52(n1), 60, 79-80, 90-91
   time spent in electorate,
      34-35
   and traditional roles of
      leadership, 45-51
   use of time, 23-25
Mezey, Michael, 1, 2, 3, 4
   30(n1), (n2), 33, 34, 58
   133
Mill, John Stuart, 3
Miller, Warren E., 4
Ministers. See Cabinet
   ministers
Mohapatra, Manindra Kumar, 2
Moors. See Sri Lanka Moors
Mukkuvar caste, 16
Muslims, 15. See also Sri
   Lanka Moors
Musolf, Lloyd, 125

Nalava caste, 16
Namasivayam, S., 82
Narain, Iqbal, 30(n5)
Nugawela, L., 49

Oberst, Robert, 7, 40, 71(n9),
   92, 98, 129, 137
Official Language Act, 139
Ong, Michael, 2

Palla caste, 16
Paraya caste, 16
Parliamentary debates, 89-94

Parliamentary debates (cont'd)
  constituent orientation,
    92-93
  and formal authority, 89-92
  rebels, 90-91
Parliamentary group meetings,
    77-81
Particularized Demands. See
    Political demands
Patronage, 58-60, 112-114,
    119(n8), 141
Patron-clientism, 45, 53(n16),
    60-61
Patterson, Samuel, 3
Perera,
  Jayantha, 64
  N.M., 94(n13)
Pfaffenberger, Brian, 16,
    21(n12)
Phadnis, Urmilla, 38, 39, 40
Pitkin, Hannah, 5, 8, 123-124
Political authority. See
    Decentralized budget
Political brokers, 62-64
Political Demands, 4-5, 33-37,
    44
  Generalized, 33-34, 36-37, 44
  Particularized, 33-34, 36,
    43, 44
  Types, 33-34
Political participation, 37-38,
    45-46
  and elections, 51
  and political stability, 1-2,
    134-136
Political parties,
  competitveness, 56-57
  local branches, 42, 104-108
  party system, 18
  and trade unions, 30(n3)
Political stability, 1-2,
    134-136
Powell, G. Bingham, 38
Premadasa, Ranasinghe, 15,
    21(n11)
Presidential powers, 17,
    21(n11), 48, 94(n1)
Presidential system. See
    Constitutions, 1978
Price, H. Douglas, 130(n)
Prime minister's powers, 21(n11)
Private members' bills, 74,
    88-89

Proportional Representation,
    20(n), 21(n14), 65,
    71(n9), 128-130,
  impact on representation, 6,
    128-130,
Provinces, number interviewed
    and seats in parliament, 12
Puri, Sashi Lata, 30(n5), 71(n4)
Pye, Lucien, 1, 2, 9(n22)

Question time, 85-88

Rae, Douglas, 7, 129
Ratnapala, Nandasena, 109,
    114-115
Rebels, See Members of
    parliament, rebels
Referendum, 19, 21(n2), 22(n17)
Religion, 14-15
Representation, 1-9
  conceptualization, 3-5,
    10(n5)
  in South Asia, 2
  in Third World, 2
  and United States Congress,
    2, 4, 9(n2), 8, 130(n)
    131(n2)
Representation theory, 1-9,
    121-128, 130
  and proportional
    representation, 128-130
Robinson, Marguerite S., 109-110
Role theory, 10(n4), 122
Roll call behavior, 2
Rondinelli, Dennis A., 137
Rothman, Jay, 136
Rural development societies, 42,
    104-107, 108,
  leadership of, 109-110
Rush, Michael, 71(n4)
Ryan, Bryce, 15, 109, 119(n6),

Salagama caste, 15-16
Samaraweera, Vijaya, 47
Scott, James C., 53(n16)
Senanayake, Dudley, 78
Shannon, Wayne W., 4, 5
Sinhala, 13, 15, 21(n6), 138-139
  official language issue,
    138-139
Sinhalese, 13, 15, 20, 139-140
  strength of ethnic identity,
    13

Simon, Herbert A., 6-7
Singer, Marshall, viii, 137
Single-member electoral constituency. See Proportional representation
Siriwardane, C.D.S., 48
Smith, Donald E., 39
Soulbury Constitution. See Constitutions, Soulbury
South Vietnam, 52(n14)
Sri Lanka Freedom Party (SLFP), 12, 18, 19-20, 50-51, 56-57, 66, 74, 78, 84, 89, 94(n4), 101, 102, 108, 118(n2)
Sri Lanka Moors 14, 21n7, 91-92
Sri Lanka Tamils 13-14, 19, 20, 21(n7), 91-92, 118(n3), 136, 138-142
    conflict with Sinhalese, 136, 138-142
    Jaffna Tamils and leadership 118(n3)
    MPs' role as mediators, 136
Stokes, Donald E., 4
Styskal, Richard A., 23
Subasinghe, D.W., 56

Tamil,
    official language issue, 138-139, 141
    See also Sri Lanka Tamils; and Indian Tamils
Tamil Congress (TC), 12, 19, 84, 91, 94(n4), 136, 141
Tamil United Liberation Front, (TULF), 12, 19, 84, 85, 92, 101-103, 136, 138, 140, 141-142
    expulsion from parliament, 19, 141-142
    See also Federal Party
Thondaman, Sauvmiamoorthy, 14, 21(n8), 48
Tigers, 138, 142

Trade unions. See Interest groups
Turner, Julius, 3

Unemployment, 57-58, 64-66, 139-140
    growth and MPs, 57-58
    as issue in Tamil-Sinhala conflict, 139-140
United National Party (UNP), 12, 18-20, 53(n17), 66, 71(n12), (n13), 84, 94(n4), 97, 101, 102, 103, 108
United States Congress, 2, 3
    and representation 2, 53(n18), 130(n), 131(n2)
Urban domination of society, 136-138

Vellala caste, 16, 21n
Verner, Joel, 133

Wahlke, John C., 5
Wahumpara caste, 16, 114
Wanigaratne, R.D., 64, 109, 111
Wedderburn, M.M., 47
Weerasooria, Wickreme, 65, 115
Weerawardena, I.D.S., 107
Weinbaum, Marvin G., 2, 9(n3)
Weiner, Myron, 39
Welikala, G.H.F., 109
Wickremeratne, L.A., 47
Wight, Martin, 45, 53(n18)
Wilson, A. Jeyaratnam, 19, 52(n1), 71(n8), 77-78, 80, 81, 94(n1), 108
Wiswa Warnapala, W.A., 22(n18), 80, 81
Wood, Leonard, 46, 48
Woodward, Calvin A., 78, 107, 119(n8)
Wriggins, W. Howard, 38, 39, 40, 77, 107

Ziegler, Harmon 23

Augsburg College
George Sverdrup Library
Minneapolis, Minnesota 55454